DECIDUOUS GARDEN TREES
AND SHRUBS

DECIDUOUS GARDEN TREES AND SHRUBS

IN COLOUR

English Editor: ANTHONY HUXLEY

Text adapted by DENIS HARDWICKE
and ALAN R. TOOGOOD

Illustrations by Verner Hancke

LONDON
BLANDFORD PRESS

First published in the English edition 1973
English text © 1973 Blandford Press Ltd.,
167 High Holborn, London WC1V 6PH

World Copyright © 1972
Politikens Forlag A/S
Copenhagen

ISBN 0 7137 0622 8

Colour section printed in Denmark by F. E. Bording A/S
Text set in Photon Times 9 pt by
Richard Clay (The Chaucer Press) Ltd., Bungay, Suffolk
and printed in Great Britain by
Fletcher & Son Ltd., Norwich

CONTENTS

FOREWORD

This book will be of considerable value to all gardeners, horticulturists and nurserymen both as a book of reference and as a guide in selecting and cultivating deciduous trees and shrubs.

Some of the colour illustrations give the trees and shrubs in their autumn colouring, and there are also scale drawings showing the growth in cultivation of the subjects.

The general introduction sets out the various uses of the trees, shrubs, climbers and roses, and includes those suitable as specimen plants, for hedging and for growing in particular situations, such as town or coastal gardens. There is also information on planting, pruning and trimming, pests and diseases.

The plates are arranged alphabetically according to the Latin names of the plants which are reproduced with the dimensional ratio of 3 : 5. They are followed by the descriptive and cultural notes, which follow the same system of numbering. Some additional subjects are included which are not numbered. The descriptions give the name of the genus and species/variety, habitat, height and form of growth in cultivation and other information.

Where English and American common names exist, these are given as well as the Latin names, which have been brought up to date in accordance with Hillier's *Manual of Trees and Shrubs*.

The selection of the plants have been made by the landscape architect Eigil Kiaer. The editor of the English edition of this and the companion volume *Evergreen Garden Trees and Shrubs* is Anthony Huxley. The text has been prepared by Alan R. Toogood and Denis Hardwicke.

SOME USES OF DECIDUOUS TREES, SHRUBS, CLIMBERS AND ROSES

Most of the plants described in this book will form permanent features in a garden, and some, such as the ornamental cherries, the crab apples and the magnolias, have a very long life indeed. The plants in this book are deciduous, that is, they shed their leaves in the autumn and renew them in the spring, unlike the evergreens which retain their foliage all through the year.

Deciduous trees and shrubs, together with the evergreens, are used to form the permanent framework of a garden. Within this framework one grows any other plants desired, such as herbaceous perennials, bulbs, alpines, annuals and so on. The trees and shrubs, once they attain reasonable proportions, give the garden a mature appearance. Most other kinds of plants cannot provide this in quite the same way.

For a well-balanced garden it is necessary to use both evergreen and deciduous trees and shrubs. By using only evergreens the planting scheme would appear very 'heavy' and sombre; while if nothing but deciduous plants were used it would be very bare in winter. A good balance is 50 per cent of each.

There is such a wide range of deciduous trees and shrubs available nowadays that it is possible to find subjects suitable for the smallest modern garden or the largest estate. For example, the fastigiate or columnar forms of some trees take up little room widthways and therefore are ideally suited to those with limited space.

Deciduous trees and shrubs can provide many interesting features: attractive summer foliage, colourful winter stems, showy flowers, fragrance, berries or fruits, and autumn tints. Some plants contribute a number of these characteristics and these are known as 'dual-purpose' plants. Good examples are *Prunus cerasifera* 'Pissardii' (138) and *Rhododendron luteum* (159).

For those who may be wondering what the difference is between a tree and a shrub, here is a simple explanation. A tree has been defined as any woody plant with a distinct trunk or main stem, and a shrub as an ornamental plant with woody stems and branches but without a tree-like trunk. A shrub may be any size from a few centimetres (inches) to 2 or 3 m (6 to 10 ft) or more when fully grown.

Some deciduous trees and shrubs look very well when grown as specimen plants, or isolated from other subjects, as then their beauty of form can be fully appreciated. There are various attractive forms among trees and shrubs, such as weeping, columnar, broadly pyramidal, rounded, flat-topped and spreading. Probably trees contribute the greater number of subjects for this particular purpose.

Specimen plants can be grown in a lawn in their own circular bed. It is not usually a good idea to take the grass right up to the trunk or stem as this can stunt the growth of the specimen, and in any case the grass may then be difficult to cut with a mower. Even small gardens could have a lawn specimen if the gardener chose one of the fastigiate forms of tree. Isolated subjects can be used to give height where needed or to provide some special focal point in a garden. It may be, for example, that you would like to plant a well-shaped shrub on the inside bend of a path to conceal the view and so create an element of surprise in your garden. There are numerous possibilities, but here are some examples of trees and shrubs which are shapely enough to make pleasing specimens:

Weeping habit—*Betula pendula* 'Dalecarlica' (20), *Betula pendula* 'Tristis' (21), *Betula pendula* 'Youngii' (22), *Fagus sylvatica* 'Pendula' (77), *Prunus* 'Kiku-shidare Sakura' (141), *Salix* × *chrysocoma* (167).

Columnar habit—*Populus nigra* 'Italica' (132), *Prunus* 'Amanogawa' (145).

Pyramidal habit—*Corylus avellana* 'Contorta' (45), *Davidia involucrata* (64), *Gleditsia triacanthos* (84), *Sorbus aria* (175).

Rounded habit—the majority come in this category, including the really large trees which are only suitable for the largest gardens and estates: *Aesculus* × *carnea* (9), *Aesculus hippocastanum* (10), *Ailanthus altissima* (11), *Aralia elata* (15), *Betula pubescens* (23), *Carpinus betulus* (29), *Castanea sativa* (31), *Catalpa bignonioides* (32), *Cladrastis lutea* (38), *Fagus sylvatica* (74–76), *Juglans regia* (95), *Laburnum* × *watereri* (98), *Liriodendron tulipifera* (103), *Magnolia stellata* (113), *Malus* (114–119), *Paulownia tomentosa* (123), *Prunus cerasifera* (138), *Prunus* 'Shirotae' (140), *Prunus dulcis* (143), *Prunus subhirtella* (147), *Pterocarya fraxinifolia* (149), *Quercus* (151–153), *Robinia pseudoacacia* (165), *Sorbus* (176–179), *Tilia platyphyllos* (197).

Flat-topped spreading habit—*Acer japonicum* (2), *Acer japonicum* 'Aconitifolium' (3), *Acer palmatum* 'Atropurpureum' (5), *Acer palmatum* 'Dissectum Ornatum' (6), *Crataegus oxyacantha* and varieties (54–56),

Mespilus germanica (120), *Morus nigra* (121), *Rhus typhina* 'Laciniata' (161), *Viburnum tomentosum* 'Mariesii' (202).

TREES AND SHRUBS WITH ATTRACTIVE FRUITS

Some shrubs and trees produce attractive berries or fruits after the flowers and these often make a brilliant show in the autumn provided the birds leave them alone. There is usually little that can be done to prevent bird attack, except, perhaps, to spray the plant with one of the proprietary bird repellents. Here is a selection of good berrying subjects:

Berberis aggregata (16), *Berberis parvifolia* (17), *Berberis thunbergii* (18), *Callicarpa japonica* (26), *Chaenomeles japonica* (35), *Chaenomeles speciosa* and *C.s.* 'Nivalis' (36–37), *Cotoneaster* (48–51), *Crataegus* 52–54 and 57), *Decaisnea fargesii* (65), *Euonymus europaeus* (71), *Hippophae rhamnoides* (89), *Lonicera* (104–107), *Malus* (114–119), *Mespilus germanica* (120), *Morus nigra* (121), *Prunus cerasifera* 'Pissardii' (138), *Prunus spinosa* (146), *Pyracantha coccinea* (150), *Rhus typhina* 'Laciniata' (161), *Sambucus* (171–173), *Sorbus* (175–179), *Symphoricarpos rivularis* (184), *Viburnum lantana* (200), *Rosa helenae* (211), *Rosa moyesii* (212), *Rosa omeiensis pteracantha* (214), *Rosa rubrifolia* (215), *Rosa rugosa* (216), *Rosa rugosa* 'Frau Dagmar Hastrup' (217), *Rosa rugosa* 'Stella Polaris' (218), *Rosa blanda* (219), *Rosa gallica* (220), *Rosa multiflora* (222), *Rosa pendulina* (223), *Rosa spinosissima* (224), *Rosa spinosissima* 'Frühlingsmorgen' (226), *Celastrus scandens* (283), *Vitis vinifera* (301–302).

FOR WINTER EFFECT

Although many plants drop their leaves in the autumn, this does not necessarily render them uninteresting. Some of them bloom during autumn and winter (every garden should have at least one or two winter-flowering shrubs), while others sport colourful or attractive bark, or create interesting silhouettes with their branches against the grey winter sky.

Bark—*Betula* (20–23), *Cornus alba* 'Sibirica' (41), *Cornus alba* 'Elegantissima' (42), *Platanus* (126–127), *Salix acutifolia* (166), *Salix* × *chrysocoma* (167), *Rosa rubrifolia* (215).

Interesting Branches—*Corylus avellana* 'Contorta' (45), *Mespilus germanica* (120), *Morus nigra* (121), *Rhus typhina* 'Laciniata' (161), *Salix matsudana* 'Tortuosa' (169).

Flowers—*Chaenomeles* (35–37), *Cornus mas* (43), *Corylopsis willmottiae* (44), *Daphne mezereum* (63), *Forsythia* × *intermedia* (79), *Hamamelis japonica* (86), *Hamamelis mollis* (87), *Magnolia stellata* (113), *Prunus subhirtella* (147), *Prunus spinosa* (146), *Jasminum nudiflorum* (291).

The leaves of some shrubs and trees take on colourful tints before they fall, and this is an invaluable characteristic in a plant. Here is a selection of subjects which colour well:

Acer campestre (1), *Acer japonicum* (2), *Acer japonicum* 'Aconitifolium' (3), *Acer palmatum* 'Atropurpureum' (5), *Acer palmatum* 'Dissectum Ornatum' (6), *Acer platanoides* (7), *Amelanchier laevis* (14), *Berberis* (16–19), *Betula* (20–23), *Cercidiphyllum japonicum* (34), *Cladrastis lutea* (38), *Clethra alnifolia* (39), *Cotinus coggygria* (47), *Cotoneaster* (48–50), *Crataegus prunifolia* (57), *Enkianthus campanulatus* (70), *Euonymus europaeus* (71), *Fothergilla major* (78), *Hamamelis japonica* (86), *Hamamelis mollis* (87), *Liriodendron tulipifera* (103), *Populus alba* (128), *Populus canescens* (130), *Populus tremula* (133), *Prunus avium* 'Plena' (144), *Prunus subhirtella* (147), *Quercus borealis* (151), *Rhododendron* (154–160), *Rhus typhina* 'Laciniata' (161), *Ribes odoratum* (163), *Sorbus* (175–176 and 178–179), *Viburnum carlesii* (199), *Viburnum lantana* (200), *Viburnum opulus* 'Sterile' (201), *Celastrus scandens* (283), *Parthenocissus* (297–298), *Vitis vinifera* (301–302).

TREES AND SHRUBS FOR HEDGING

Some trees and shrubs make good formal hedges because they can be regularly trimmed closely with shears. Those with attractive flowers or berries are not usually clipped hard otherwise they will not bloom or produce their fruits. Instead, these are best grown as informal hedges or, if a little clipping is desired, as semi-formal hedges.

For Formal Hedges. *Carpinus betulus* (29), *Crataegus monogyna* (52), *Crataegus oxyacantha* (54–56), *Fagus sylvatica* (74), *Fagus sylvatica purpurea* (75), *Ligustrum ovalifolium* 'Aureum' (101), *Ligustrum vulgare* (102), *Punus cerasifera* 'Pissardii' (138), *Pyracantha coccinea* (150)—often grown as a formal hedge even though most of the berries are lost.

For Informal or Semi-formal Hedges. *Berberis* (16–19), *Crataegus monogyna* (52), *Crataegus oxyacantha* (54–56), *Forsythia intermedia* (79), *Fuchsia* 'Riccartonii' (82), *Potentilla fruticosa* (135–137), *Pyracantha coccinea* (150), *Rhododendron* (154–160), *Symphoricarpos rivularis* (184), *Tamarix pentandra* (196), *Rosa moyesii* (212), *Rosa* 'Nevada' (213), *Rosa omeiensis pteracantha* (214), *Rosa rugosa* (216–218), Rose 'Queen Elizabeth' (230), Rose 'Chinatown' (239), Rose 'Peace' (262).

RECOMMENDED FOR TOWN ATMOSPHERE

In big towns, especially industrial towns, the atmosphere is usually polluted and is not generally considered conducive to good gardening. However, there are quite a few trees and shrubs which will grow well in such conditions. Of the two, deciduous plants are probably better than evergreens because they drop their leaves each autumn, by which time they are usually covered with grime, and produce fresh new ones in spring, whereas evergreens can look perpetually dirty unless they are washed off occasionally. The following trees and shrubs are recommended for a polluted town atmosphere:

Acer platanoides (7), *Acer pseudoplatanus* (8), *Aesculus* (9–10), *Ailanthus altissima* (11), *Alnus* (12–13), *Amelanchier laevis* (14), *Aralia elata* (15), *Berberis* (16–19), *Betula* (20–23), *Buddleia davidii* (24), *Carpinus betulus* (29), *Catalpa bignonioides* (32), *Ceanothus* × *delilianus* (33), *Chaenomeles* (35–37), *Clethra alnifolia* (39), *Colutea arborescens* (40), *Cornus alba* (41–42), *Cotoneaster* (48–51), *Crataegus* (52–57), *Cytissus* (58–62), *Daphne mezereum* (63), *Davidia involucrata* (64), *Deutzia* (66–68), *Fagus* (74–77), *Forsythia* × *intermedia* (79), *Fraxinus* (80–81), *Genista tinctoria* (83), *Hibiscus syriacus* (88), *Hydrangea macrophylla* (90–91), *Hypericum beanii* (93), *Kerria japonica* 'Pleniflora' (96), *Laburnum* × *watereri* (98), *Ligustrum ovalifolium* (101), *Liriodendron tulipifera* (103), *Lycium barbarum* (108), *Magnolia* × *soulangeana* (111–112), *Magnolia stellata* (113), *Malus* (114–119), *Mespilus germanica* (120), *Morus nigra* (121), *Philadelphus* (124–125), *Platanus* (126–127), *Populus* (128–133), *Prunus cerasifera* 'Pissardii' (138), *Prunus padus* (139), *Prunus* 'Shirotae' (140), *Prunus* 'Kiku-shidare Sakura' (141), *Prunus dulcis* (143), *Prunus avium* 'Plena' (144), *Prunus* 'Amanogawa' (145), *Pterocarya fraxinifolia* (149), *Pyracantha coccinea* (150), *Rhododendron* (154–160), *Rhus typhina* 'Laciniata' (161), *Ribes* (162–164), *Robinia pseudoacacia* (165), *Salix* (166–170), *Sambucus canadensis* (171), *Sambucus nigra* (172), *Sorbaria arborea* (174), *Sorbus aria* (175), *Sorbus aucuparia* (176), *Spiraea* (180–183), *Symphoricarpos rivularis* (184), *Syringa* (185–195), *Tilia platyphyllos* (197), *Ulmus glabra* (198), *Viburnum* (199–202), *Weigela* (203–206), *Rosa* (208–279), *Jasminum nudiflorum* (291), *Parthenocissus* (297–298), *Wisteria sinensis* (300).

SUITABLE FOR SHADE

The following subjects are suitable for a sunless or partially sunless position which is, however, reasonably open (not overhung by large dense trees, for example):

Berberis (16–19), part shade; *Chaenomeles* (35–37), for north or east walls; *Corylopsis willmottiae* (44), part shade; *Cotoneaster* (48–51), part shade; *Daphne mezereum* (63), part shade; *Enkianthus campanulatus* (70), part shade; *Hydrangea* (90–92), dappled shade; *Ligustrum* (100–102), *Pyracantha coccinea* (150), good on north or east wall; *Rhododendron*

(154–160), partial shade; *Ribes* (162–164), *Symphoricarpos rivularis* (184), *Viburnum opulus* 'Sterile' (201), partial shade; *Celastrus scandens* (283), for north or east wall; *Clematis* (284–289), a northern aspect is suitable; *Hydrangea petiolaris* (290), excellent for north or east wall; *Jasminum nudiflorum* (291), grows well on north or east wall; *Lonicera* (292–296), thrives in semi-shade; *Parthenocissus* (297), for north or east walls.

RECOMMENDED FOR COASTAL PLANTING

These plants will tolerate exposed maritime areas with their high, salt-laden winds:

Colutea arborescens (40), *Crataegus* (52–57), *Elaeagnus commutata* (67), *Fuchsia* 'Riccartonii' (82), *Hippophae rhamnoides* (89), *Lycium barbarum* (108), *Populus alba* (128), *Populus canescens* (130), *Populus tremula* (133), *Prunus spinosa* (146), *Sorbus aria* (175), *Sorbus aucuparia* (176), *Tamarix pentandra* (196), *Rosa rugosa* (216–218).

SOME USES FOR CLIMBERS

Climbing plants can be used to drape walls, fences and screens, and to cover arches, pergolas and arbours. There are some which can be allowed to scramble up into trees or to cover large tree stumps. Yet others are suitable for covering unsightly sheds and outbuildings.

The method of climbing must be known when planting so that suitable support can be given. Some, like *Parthenocissus* (297–298), are completely self-supporting—they attach themselves to walls by means of adhesive pads on the ends of tendrils. Others need something extra to grip such as trellis or horizontal wires fixed to the wall. Examples here are the *Clematis* (284–289). Then there are twining plants which can lash themselves around poles, trees, columns and so on, typical of these being the *Lonicera* (292–296).

Climbing plants are especially useful in small gardens where there is plenty of vertical space but limited horizontal space. It is surprising how infrequently the former is utilised by amateur gardeners!

USING ROSES

The shrub roses (208–226) are easily accommodated in most gardens as the best place to grow them is in a shrub or mixed border. They associate well with most other shrubs and perennial plants. A rather nice idea, if you want to give them a bed or border on their own, is to underplant them with Lenten Roses, Helleborus orientalis hybrids. These will give colour and interest early in the year before the roses are in bloom.

Floribunda roses can also be planted in a shrub or mixed border as their flowers are sufficiently informal not to look out of place. Or they can be grown in their own beds where their sheer abundance of blooms will make a superb show throughout the summer and into the autumn.

In the estimation of most gardeners the only way to grow the hybrid teas with their beautifully formal flowers is in beds on their own—in a formal rose garden if there is sufficient space. They certainly do not mix easily with most other plants.

If you grow floribundas and hybrid teas in their own beds it is a good idea to grow evergreen ground-cover plants between them to hide the soil during the winter, when the roses are nothing more than bare sticks. Blue-flowered plants seem to associate best of all with roses, such as the Periwinkle (*Vinca minor*), *Campanula poscharskyana*, *Viola labradorica*, *Viola cornuta* and *Campanula portenschlagiana*. All bloom during summer.

To get the best effect from beds of hybrid teas or floribundas, grow only one variety per bed, if space allows, that is. This is usually more satisfying than many colours in one bed.

PLANTING

The first thing to consider is the type of soil in your garden. As stressed in the descriptive list, some trees and shrubs (such as azaleas) will only grow in acid soils and if your soil is limy it is no use trying to grow them.

To get a tree or shrub off to a good start it is necessary to dig the soil thoroughly before planting. Dig to two depths of the spade but do not bring the subsoil up to the surface. While digging, thoroughly mix well-rotted manure, good garden compost or garden peat in with the soil, especially if the ground is poor and sandy or thin and chalky. Then in the topsoil mix in a dressing of bonemeal at 120 gm per square metre (4 oz per square yard). Try to prepare the ground a few weeks before planting to allow it time to settle.

When digging, remove any perennial weeds as these are more difficult to control once shrubs have been planted. The roots of perennial weeds must be picked out. If the ground is very badly infested it may be a good idea to apply paraquat weedkiller to kill them before digging commences. As regrowth is very likely it will be necessary to give a repeat application a few weeks later. Apply according to the maker's directions on the packet.

Container-grown trees and shrubs can be planted at any time of the year so long as the ground is not frozen or waterlogged. These must be carefully removed from their containers to avoid disturbing the rootball. Each one is placed in a hole slightly larger than the rootball, fine soil is worked well into the surrounding gap and the plant is firmed thoroughly with your heels. After planting, the top of the rootball should be very slightly below the soil surface.

Bare-root subjects lifted from a nursery are planted only in the dormant season from November to March. They need to be planted in a hole sufficiently large to allow their roots to be spread out to their full extent. Fine soil is then worked between and over them, firming with the heels as you proceed. Never plant trees and shrubs any deeper than they were in the nursery—the soil mark on the stem is the guide.

When planting a tree it is wise to give it support with a wooden stake for a few years until well established. The stake should be put in position in the middle of the hole before planting. It should be sufficiently long so that after it has been driven well into the soil, the top reaches the lowermost branches of the tree. Use proprietary tree ties, placing one at the top of the stake and one or two more lower down. Check such ties regularly to ensure they are not cutting into the trunk as the tree grows. If you use the buckle type you will find these are easily adjusted as a tree thickens out.

Young trees and shrubs must be thoroughly watered whenever the soil starts to become dry, until such time as they are really well established. Many young plants in amateurs' gardens are lost because they are not watered in dry weather.

It is most important when siting a tree or shrub to bear in mind its ultimate height and spread. Too often insufficient space is allowed when planting. When planting shrubs in a bed or border the minimum distance between them should equal two-thirds of their height when fully grown. The heights are, of course, given in this book. This spacing may certainly be increased with advantage to a distance equal to the height of a mature shrub. If space allows, the best effect is gained by planting two or three shrubs of the same kind in a group.

Remember that most mature trees, except fastigiate kinds, have a branch spread roughly equal to their height; this is a good guide when planting. The ultimate heights at maturity of all the trees are given in this book.

Obviously young trees and shrubs will look somewhat lost if they are left to occupy large spaces, but one can always plant bulbs, hardy perennials or even sow annuals in the vacant ground to provide interest and colour while the more permanent trees or shrubs are developing. Once planted, trees and shrubs should remain undisturbed for the rest of their lives. They will resent being moved around so be sure to plant them in the right place at the start. This may sound obvious to many people but in some private gardens plants are moved so frequently that they give up the unequal struggle!

PRUNING AND TRIMMING

Quite a few deciduous shrubs need annual pruning to encourage a good quantity of large flowers. Some, which flower in winter, spring or early summer on wood formed the previous year, are cut back immediately after flowering. The old flowered stems are cut back to young shoots which are forming lower down. Examples of shrubs so treated are *Forsythia*, *Weigela*, *Deutzia* and *Philadelphus*. Some other shrubs which flower later in the summer on wood produced during the current year, have all their stems cut back hard (almost to ground level) in March or April. Examples are *Buddleia davidii* and *Fuchsia* 'Riccartonii'.

Other shrubs need nothing more than the removal of dead flower heads to prevent seed production which can have a weakening effect. Chief among these are *Rhododendrons* and *Syringa*, also roses where hips are not a feature.

Dead or dying wood should be removed from all shrubs and trees whenever necessary. Very congested and/or very weak growth should also be thinned out, preferably in the winter. Any cuts over $2\frac{1}{2}$ cm (1 in.) in diameter should be painted with a proprietary bituminous tree paint. Ornamental plums, peaches and cherries should only be pruned in June or July, to prevent infection from silver-leaf disease.

Formal hedges will need clipping in the summer to keep them neat and tidy. Informal hedges need only an occasional looking over to cut back the odd straggly or badly placed shoot. Hard clipping of flowering or berrying hedges will result in loss of their main attraction.

PESTS AND DISEASES

Although there are many kinds of insect pest that will attack deciduous trees and shrubs, such as caterpillars, aphids, capsid bugs, froghoppers, leaf miners, weevils and red spider mites, these are unlikely to cause more than temporary disfigurement, and attacked trees and shrubs usually get over such trouble. In any case there is not much that can be done for large trees. It is in the first few years after planting that insect attack can cripple trees and shrubs, and a watch should be kept on them; they will still be small enough for spraying with an appropriate insecticide to be effective. A broad-spectrum insecticide, perhaps containing BHC, malathion and the systemic rogor, should deal with almost any insect pest. Sevin dust will control caterpillars.

If rabbits or deer are known to be in your locality and likely to enter the garden, the trunks of trees must be protected, or these animals may gnaw the bark which is likely to kill the tree. Special wrap-around spiral protectors are readily available, or a cylinder of wire-netting can be used.

Diseases are usually caused by various kinds of fungi. Probably the most common one is mildew, especially on roses, which appears as white patches on leaves and shoots. Spray with a suitable fungicide such as one containing dinocap. Rose black spot which appears as black spots on the leaves should be rigorously controlled by spraying with captan. In Britain it is now possible to obtain a systemic soil fungicide which circulates in the sap stream of the plants and really is most effective in controlling these diseases.

Any wound over $2\frac{1}{2}$ cm (1 in.) in diameter caused by branch cutting or breaking should be painted immediately with a bituminous tree paint to prevent entry of fungus spores.

The most dreaded disease is honey fungus or *Armillaria mellea*, which can very quickly kill trees and shrubs. The fungus penetrates the roots and stems, and spreads from plant to plant by means of black bootlace-like threads. White fungal threads can also be seen beneath the bark at soil level, and groups of honey-coloured toadstools appear around the base of infected plants. There is now on the market in Britain a product called Armillatox specifically for the control of this disease. A solution of the concentrate is watered around infected plants according to the manufacturer's instructions. It is available only from Armillatox Ltd., 44 Town Street, Duffield, Derby, DE6 4GH.

DECIDUOUS TREES AND SHRUBS

1. **Acer campestre**
   Field Maple

2. **Acer japonicum**

3. **Acer japonicum** 'Aconitifolium'
   a. Fruit

4. **Acer negundo** 'Variegatum'
   Box Elder

5. **Acer palmatum**
   Japanese Maple

6. **Acer palmatum** 'Dissectum Ornatum'

7. **Acer platanoides**
   Norway Maple
   a. Fruit

8. **Acer pseudoplatanus**
   Sycamore
   a. Fruit

3   1   4-6   7   2   8

9. Aesculus hippocastanum
Common Horse Chestnut
a. Fruit
b. Flower Spike

10. Aesculus × carnea
Red Horse Chestnut

11. Ailanthus altissima
Tree of Heaven

13

13 a

14

12. Alnus glutinosa
Alder
a. Catkins

13. Alnus incana
Grey Alder
a. Ripe Fruit

14. Amelanchier laevis

12   12   14

15. Aralia elata
Japanese Angelica Tree

16. Berberis aggregata
Barberry
a. Berries

16

16 a

17

19

17. Berberis parvifolia

18. Berberis thunbergii
    (in autumn)

19. Berberis thunbergii
    'Atropurpurea'

20-21   23   22

24 c

24 b

24 a

25

24. Buddleia davidii
Butterfly Bush, Summer Lilac
a. Royal Red
b. 'Charming'
c. 'White Cloud'

26

27

25. **Buddleia globosa**
Orange Ball Tree

26. **Callicarpa japonica**
Beauty Berry

27. **Calycanthus floridus**
Carolina Allspice

28

29

28. **Caragana arborescens**
Pea Tree or Shrub

29. **Carpinus betulus**
Hornbeam

30. **Caryopteris incana**
Blue beard

30

31. Castanea sativa
Sweet Chestnut
a. Husk and three nuts
b. Ripe nut

31a

31b

32

31

32. Catalpa bignonioides
Indian Bean Tree

32   **31**

33   34

33. Ceanothus × delilianus
34. Cercidiphyllum japonicum

35. Chaenomeles japonica
Japanese Quince

36. Chaenomeles speciosa
a. Fruit

37. Chaenomeles speciosa 'Nivalis'

38. Cladrastis lutea
Yellow-wood

39. Clethra alnifolia
Sweet Pepper Bush, White Alder

40. Colutea arborescens
Bladder Senna
a. Seed Pods

41. Cornus alba 'Sibirica'
(Autumn colour)
Red-barked Dogwood

42. Cornus alba 'Elegantissima'

43. Cornus mas
Cornelian Cherry
a–b. Fruit

41

43 b

43 a

43

42

40

43

44. **Corylopsis willmottiae**

45. **Corylus avellana** 'Contorta'
Corkscrew Hazel

46. **Corylus maxima** 'Purpurea'
Purple-leaved Filbert, Hazelnut

47. **Cotinus coggygria**
Smoke Tree

48. Cotoneaster acutifolius
49. Cotoneaster divaricatus
50. Cotoneaster horizontalis
51. Cotoneaster multiflorus

58

60

59

63 a

63

61

62

64

58. **Cytisus × praecox**
Warminster Broom

59. **Cytisus × praecox** 'Allgold'

60. **Cytisus × praecox** 'Hollandia'

61. **Cytisus purpureus**
Purple Broom

62. **Cytisus purpureus** 'Incarnatus'

63. **Daphne mezereum**
Mezereum
a. Fruit

64. **Davidia involucrata**
Handkerchief Tree, Dove Tree

66

68

65

69

67

65. **Decaisnea fargesii**

66. **Deutzia × magnifica**

67. **Deutzia × rosea** 'Carminea'

68. **Deutzia scabra** 'Plena'

69. **Elaeagnus commutata**
    Silver Berry

70

72

73

71

70. Enkianthus campanulatus
Pagoda Bush

71. Euonymus europaeus
Spindle Tree

72. Exochorda racemosa
Pearl Bush

73. Ficus carica
Common Fig

74. Fagus sylvatica
   Common or European Beech
   a. Beech nut

75. Fagus sylvatica purpurea
   Purple Beech

6. Fagus sylvatica heterophylla
Fern-leaved Beech

7. Fagus sylvatica 'Pendula'
Weeping Beech

8. Fothergilla major

77   74-76

79. Forsythia × intermedia

80. Fraxinus excelsior
Ash
a. Flowering stem
b. Winged fruit

79

80 a

80 b

80

81. Fraxinus ornus
Manna or Flowering Ash

81

81   80

82

83

82. Fuchsia 'Riccartonii'
   Hardy Fuchsia

83. Genista tinctoria
   Dyer's Greenweed

84. Gleditsia tricanthos
   Honey or Sweet Locust

84

85. **Halesia carolina**
    Snowdrop Tree, Silver-Bell

86. **Hamamelis japonica**
    Japanese Witch Hazel

85

88

87. **Hamamelis mollis**
    Chinese Witch Hazel

88. **Hibiscus syriacus**
    Tree or Rose Mallow

89

90

90

89. **Hippophae rhamnoides**
Sea Buckthorn

90. **Hydrangea macrophylla**
Lacecap Hydrangea (pink flower),
Hortensia (blue flower)

93

91. **Hydrangea macrophylla**
'Bouquet Rose'

92. **Hydrangea paniculata**

93. **Hypericum beanii**

94. **Indigofera gerardiana**
Indigo

94

92

91

95. Juglans regia
Walnut
a. Nut

96. Kerria japonica 'Pleniflora'

97. Kolkwitzia amabilis
Beauty Bush

97

98

99

98. Laburnum × watereri
Golden Rain

99. Lespedeza bicolor
Bush Clover

102

102 a

100

101

100 a

100. **Ligustrum obtusifolium regelianum**
   a. Bare stem and fruit clusters

101. **Ligustrum ovalifolium** 'Aureum'
   Golden Privet

102. **Ligustrum vulgare**
   Common Privet
   a. Fruit clusters

103. **Liriodendron tulipifera**
   Tulip Tree

103

104. **Lonicera maackii**
   a. Stem and fruit

105. **Lonicera syringantha**

106. **Lonicera tatarica**

107. **Lonicera tatarica** 'Lutea'

108. **Lycium barbarum**
   Box Thorn

106

108

110

109

113

111   111 a   112

109. Magnolia obovata

110. Magnolia sieboldii

111. Magnolia × soulangeana
   a. Fruit

112. Magnolia × soulangeana 'Lennei'

113. Magnolia stellata
   Star Magnolia

114. Malus baccata
Siberian Crab Apple

115. Malus floribunda
Japanese or Showy Crab Apple
a. Fruit

117 a

114

116. **Malus** 'John Downie'
a. Fruit

117. **Malus** × **purpurea**
a. Fruit

118. **Malus** × **scheideckeri**
a. Fruit

115   114

119. **Malus halliana**

120. **Mespilus germanica**
Medlar

121. **Morus nigra**
Black Mulberry

119   121

122

122. Paeonia suffruticosa
Moutan or Tree Paeony

124

123 a

125

123

123. **Paulownia tomentosa**
a. Fruit

124. **Philadelphus coronarius**
Mock Orange

125. **Philadelphus coronarius**
'Flore Pleno'

127

126. Platanus × hispanica
Plane Tree

127. Platanus orientalis
Oriental Plane

126

127   126

128. Populus alba
White Poplar, Aspen

129. Populus × berolinensis
Berlin Poplar

130. Populus canescens
Grey Poplar

131. Populus lasiocarpa

132. Populus nigra 'Italica'
Lombardy Poplar

133 b 133 a 133

133. Populus tremula
Aspen or European Poplar
a. Male catkin
b. Female catkin

131   128   130   129   132

134

135

134. **Potentilla arbuscula**

135. **Potentilla fruticosa** 'Jackman's Variety'

136. **Potentilla fruticosa mandshurica**

137. **Potentilla fruticosa** 'Tangerine'

138. Prunus cerasifera
'Pissardii'
Purple-leaved or
Cherry Plum

142

138

139. Prunus padus
European Bird Cherry

140. Prunus 'Shirotae'
Japanese Cherry

139

141. Prunus
'Kiku-shidare Sakura'
Japanese Cherry

142. Prunus triloba
'Flore Pleno'

139   141   140

143
144
145
147
148

143. **Prunus dulcis**
Almond

144. **Prunus avium** 'Plena'
Double Gean

145. **Prunus** 'Amanogawa'
Japanese Cherry

146. Prunus spinosa
Sloe, Blackthorn
a. Fruit

147. Prunus subhirtella
Spring or Rosebud Cherry

148. Prunus tenella
Dwarf Russian Almond

149

149. Pterocarya fraxinifolia
Wing Nut

150. Pyracantha coccinea
Firethorn

150

151

153

152. **Quercus cerris**
     Turkey Oak

153. **Quercus robur**
     Common Oak
   a. Acorns

153 a

152

151. Quercus borealis
Red Oak, Northern Red Oak (in autumn)

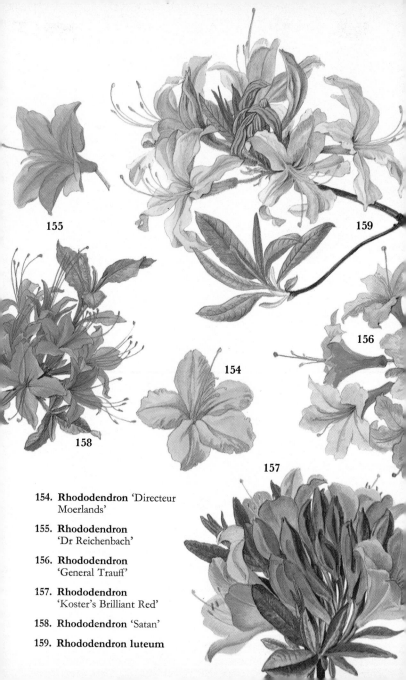

155

159

156

154

158

157

154. **Rhododendron** 'Directeur
Moerlands'

155. **Rhododendron**
'Dr Reichenbach'

156. **Rhododendron**
'General Trauff'

157. **Rhododendron**
'Koster's Brilliant Red'

158. **Rhododendron** 'Satan'

159. **Rhododendron luteum**

160. Rhododend-
ron schlippen-
bachii

161. **Rhus typhina**
'Laciniata'
Stag's-horn
Sumach

162. Ribes alpinum
Mountain Currant

163. Ribes odoratum
Buffalo Currant

164. Ribes sanguineum
Flowering Currant
a. Crimson variety

165. Robinia pseudoacacia
Common or False Acacia

165

169

166

168

166 a

170

167

167   166   168

171. Sambucus canadensis
American or Sweet Elderberry

172. Sambucus nigra
Common or European Elder

173. Sambucus racemosa
Red-berried Elder

174. Sorbaria arborea

174

173

175. Sorbus aria
Whitebeam Tree

176. Sorbus aucuparia
Rowan

177. Sorbus intermedia
Swedish Whitebeam

178. Sorbus koehneana

179. Sorbus vilmorinii

178

175

176

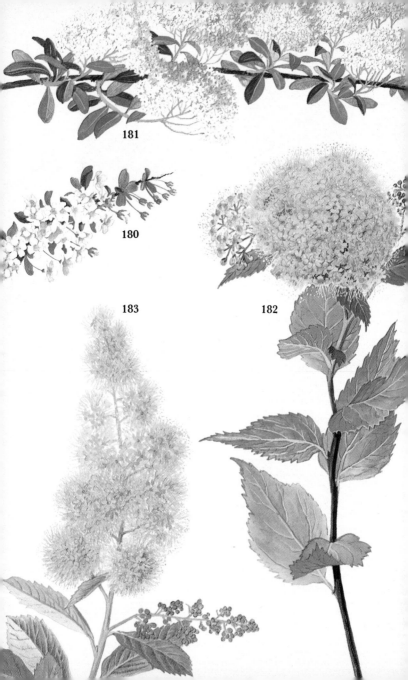

181

180

183

182

180. Spiraea × arguta
Bridal Wreath

181. Spiraea henryi

182. Spiraea japonica

184

183. Spiraea salicifolia
Bridewort

184. Symphoricarpos rivularis
Snowberry

185

189

185. **Syringa × chinensis**
Rouen Lilac

186. **Syringa microphylla**

187. **Syringa × prestoniae**
'Coral'

188. **Syringa × prestoniae**
'Nocturne'

189. **Syringa reflexa**

190. Syringa vulgaris 'Jacques Callot'
Lilac

191. Syringa vulgaris 'Madame Francisque Morel'

192. Syringa vulgaris 'Marie Legraye'

193. **Syringa vulgaris** 'Madame Lemoine'

194. **Syringa vulgaris** 'Primrose'

195. **Syringa vulgaris** 'Souvenir de Louis Spaeth'

196

197

196. **Tamarix pentandra**
Tamarisk

197. **Tilia platyphyllos**
Broad-leaved or Large-
leaved Lime

197   198

198. Ulmus glabra
Wych or Scotch Elm
a. Flower

199. Viburnum carlesii

200. Viburnum lantana
Wayfaring Tree

201. Viburnum opulus 'Sterile'
Snowball Tree, European Cranberry
Bush

202. Viburnum tomentosum 'Mariesii'
a. *V. t.* 'Sterile'
Japanese Snowball Tree

203. **Weigela** florida

204. **Weigela** 'Bristol Ruby'

205. **Weigela** florida 'Variegata'

206. **Weigela** 'Mont Blanc'

207. **Weigela** middendorffiana

SHRUB ROSES

209

211

208

210

212

208. **Rosa × alba** 'Maiden's Blush'

209. **Rosa carolina**

210. **Rosa foetida** 'Persiana'
Persian Yellow Rose

211. **Rosa helenae**
a. Hips

212. **Rosa moyesii**
a. Hips

213. **Rosa** 'Nevada'

216

218

217

215

214. **Rosa omeiensis pteracantha**
Mount Omei Rose

215. **Rosa rubrifolia**

216. **Rosa rugosa**
Ramanas Rose

217. **Rosa rugosa** 'Frau Dagmar Hastrup'
a. Hips

218. **Rosa rugosa** 'Stella Polaris'

219. **Rosa blanda**
Meadow Rose (hips)

220. **Rosa gallica**
French Rose (hips)

221. **Rosa hugonis**

222. **Rosa multiflora** (hips)

223. **Rosa pendulina** (hips)

224. **Rosa spinosissima** (hips)

225. **Rosa spinosissima** 'Frühlingsgold'

226. **Rosa spinosissima** 'Frühlingsmorgen'

HYBRID TEA AND FLORIBUNDA ROSES

238

240

246

239

241

242

244

243

245

247

248

249

251

254

247. 'Grandmère Jenny'

248. 'Hakuun'

249. 'Alexander'

250. 'Intermezzo'

251. 'Jan Spek'

252. 'Korona'

253. 'Perfecta'

254. 'Colour Wonder'

250

252

253

266

270

271

RAMBLING, CLIMBING
AND PILLAR ROSES

272

273

274

275

276

277

278. 'Sanders' White'
279. 'Sympathie'

CLIMBING PLANTS

280

280. **Actinidia kolomikta**

281. **Aristolochia durior**
Dutchman's Pipe

281

283

282

284

285

285 a

286 e

286 b

286 d

289

287

288

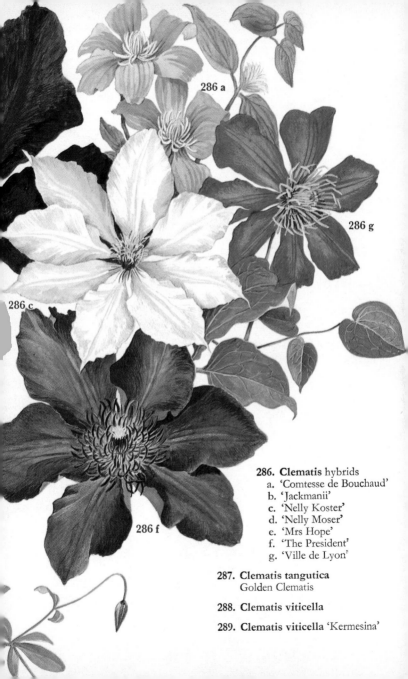

286 a

286 g

286 c

286 f

286. Clematis hybrids
   a. 'Comtesse de Bouchaud'
   b. 'Jackmanii'
   c. 'Nelly Koster'
   d. 'Nelly Moser'
   e. 'Mrs Hope'
   f. 'The President'
   g. 'Ville de Lyon'

287. Clematis tangutica
   Golden Clematis

288. Clematis viticella

289. Clematis viticella 'Kermesina'

290

291

292

290. Hydrangea petiolaris
Climbing Hydrangea

291. Jasminum nudiflorum
Winter Jasmine

292. Lonicera caprifolium
Perfoliate Honeysuckle

293. Lonicera × heckrotii

294. Lonicera henryi

295. Lonicera periclymenum
Woodbine
a. Fruit

296. Lonicera × tellmanniana

297

298

297. **Parthenocissus quinquefolia**
Virginia Creeper

298. **Parthenocissus tricuspidata**
Japanese or Boston Ivy

299. **Polygonum baldschuanicum**
Russian Vine

300. **Wisteria sinensis**
Chinese Wisteria

299

300

301. Vitis vinifera 'Black Cluster'
Grape Vine

302. Vitis vinifera 'Early Malingre'
Grape Vine

DESCRIPTIVE AND CULTURAL NOTES

1. Acer campestre
Field Maple

Height 10–15 m (33–50 ft). A common native tree in southern England on limy soil, also in Europe and western Asia. In autumn the foliage makes a fine display, varying from glowing golden-yellow to red and bronze tints. The grey bark is closely fissured and the hard, finely grained wood is excellent for cabinet making. An attractive tree for a garden on chalky soil which may also be planted to form a dense hedge or screen. Propagate from seed.

2. Acer japonicum

Height up to 6 m (20 ft). A small tree or large bush from Japan with drooping clusters of red flowers which appear with the unfurling of soft green leaves. The finely cut leaves turn brilliant crimson in autumn. There are several most decorative forms such as the slow-growing 'Aureum' with pale golden-yellow leaves that retain their colour throughout the season. Seen at its best in partial shade. These maples like a well drained, moist soil and a position sheltered from bleak winds. Propagate by layering.

3. Acer japonicum 'Aconitifolium'

This form is also known as 'Laciniatum' or 'Filicifolium'. The deeply cut and fern-like leaves turn rich crimson in the autumn. Propagate by layering.

4. Acer negundo
Box Elder

Height 6–9 m (20–30 ft). A fast-growing tree of wide-spreading habit from North America. The young shoots and leaves are bright green. Does well in any well drained, moist soil. Propagate from seed. More decorative are the variegated forms such as the outstanding 'Variegatum' with broad, irregular white margin to the light green leaves. This is liable to revert to the type and any growths that show this tendency should be cut away. It is propagated by grafting on to seedlings of the type plant.

5. Acer palmatum 'Atropurpureum'
Japanese Maple

Height up to 5 m (16 ft). A native of Japan and central China forming a rounded head of bright green five- or seven-lobed leaves. *A. palmatum* and its many forms tolerate chalk but do best in neutral or acid soil of good depth. Hardy, but liable to damage by spring frost, so plant in a sheltered position. 'Atropurpureum' is one of the most popular of the Japanese maples with bronze-red leaves throughout the summer. Propagate by layering.

6. Acer palmatum 'Dissectum Ornatum'
Japanese Maple

Height up to 3 m (10 ft). Makes a neat, mushroom-shaped shrub with finely divided bronze leaves on arching stems. There are several other attractive forms with finely cut green or purple foliage. Propagate by layering.

7. Acer platanoides
Norway Maple

Height up to 18 m (60 ft). A fast-growing European tree with attractive greenish-yellow flowers in clusters that appear in April before the fresh green leaves which turn clear yellow in the autumn. Easily raised from seed. Outstanding forms are 'Crimson King' with crimson-purple leaves and 'Drummondii' with white margins to the leaves. These dark-foliage forms are most effective when planted in an open sunny position. Propagate by grafting on to stocks of type plant.

8. Acer pseudoplatanus
Sycamore

Height up to 25 m (80 ft). Of European origin, naturalised in Britain. The dull green leaves are pale grey beneath and the dense tassels of yellowish-green flowers appear with the leaves in late spring. In autumn the leaves turn a dull yellow or brown, but are frequently disfigured by tar-spot fungus. It is liable to seed itself too freely in gardens but is useful to form a shelter-belt in exposed coastal districts. There are numerous forms with purple, yellowish-green or variegated foliage which are more decorative for the garden where space permits.

9. Aesculus hippocastanum
Common Horse Chestnut

Height up to 30 m (100 ft). A fast-growing, wide-spreading tree from the Balkans which makes a grand show in May with its large conical heads of white flowers, likened to candles. These are followed by large spiny fruits which open in autumn to expose one, or occasionally two, attractive brown seeds, known as conkers to generations of children. These can be used for propagation. This large tree is more suitable for a park than a garden. Its dense foliage throws a deep shade and the wide-spreading surface roots make it difficult to grow other plants within its compass.

10. Aesculus × carnea
Red Horse Chestnut

Height up to 15 m (50 ft). A hybrid of unknown origin. Makes a large round-headed tree bearing rose-pink panicles of flower in May and June. Makes a splendid specimen tree but requires ample space to spread and be seen at its best. Hardy in most parts of the British Isles and easily cultivated in any soil. Propagate from seed.

11. Ailanthus altissima
Tree of Heaven

Height up to 20 m (65 ft). This fast-growing Chinese species thrives best in a light, well-drained soil of good depth and does well in town gardens. On young trees the handsome ash-like foliage is up to 1 m (3 ft) in length. The greenish-yellow male and female flowers are borne on separate trees, the female tree producing in the autumn large bunches of reddish-brown fruit. Propagate from seed.

12. Alnus glutinosa
Alder

Height up to 25 m (80 ft). A common tree in the British Isles and widespread in Europe, quick-growing in wet ground beside streams, lakes and marshes. Also to be found in North Africa and western Asia. The catkins are formed in summer and mature in the following spring. The fissured bark is dark sooty-brown, and the wood was at one time used for clog-making. Can be raised from seed.

13. Alnus incana
Grey Alder

Height 15–20 m (60–65 ft). From northern and central Europe, Caucasus and eastern North America. Differs from he common alder in its smooth grey bark, pointed leaves which are greyish and with more regularly serrated margin. These are not glutinous in the young stage, as in *A. glutinosa*. This extremely hardy tree is naturalised in Britain and is useful for wet soils. Propagate from seed.

14. Amelanchier laevis

Height up to 6 m (20 ft). This North American species is often confused with *A. canadensis*, the Snowy Mespilus. The leaves of *A. laevis* are not downy and they are more purplish red in spring and are charming with the fragrant white flowers in early May. The autumn foliage is brilliant red and yellow tinted and the purplish-black fruit has a sweet flavour. For sun or partial shade and a moist, lime free soil. Propagate from seed sown in cold frame as soon as ripe.

15. Aralia elata
Japanese Angelica Tree

Height up to 4 m (13 ft). This Japanese species has exceptionally large leaves about 1 m (3 ft) in length, yet they have a graceful, airiness and colour in the autumn. Panicles of white flowers are produced in early autumn. Thrives in a well-drained loam and in shade. Should be planted towards the back of a shrub or herbaceous border to mask the somewhat bare stems. In some soils it is liable to sucker. It can be propagated from suckers.

16. Berberis aggregata
Barberry

Height 1·5 m (5 ft). This Chinese species makes a dense shrub with arching stems of yellow flowers in July followed by a heavy crop of long-lasting berries and autumn-tinted leaves. In common with other berberis this thrives

in ordinary garden soil and tolerates shallow, poor soil, in sun or partial shade. Propagate all berberis from seed or cuttings.

17. Berberis parvifolia

Height up to 1 m (3 ft). A western Chinese shrub of dome-shaped or semi-prostrate habit making it suitable for growing on a bank or large rock garden. The small leaves turn purplish in winter. Closely related to *B. wilsonae*.

18. Berberis thunbergii

Height $1\frac{1}{2}$–2 m (5–6 ft). A Japanese shrub remarkable for its autumn foliage and bright red berries. There are several different forms and named varieties.

19. Berberis thunbergii
'Atropurpurea'

Height 2 m (6 ft). Somewhat taller than the type with striking reddish-purple leaves throughout the spring and summer. 'Atropurpurea Nana' is a dwarf form about 60 cm (2 ft) in height suitable for a heather bed or rock garden.

20. Betula pendula 'Dalecarlica'
Swedish Birch

Height up to 20 m (65 ft). A tall, graceful weeping form of the European Silver Birch with long pendent branches and deeply cut, fern-like leaves. Makes an admirable specimen tree and in common with other birches it associates happily with hardy heathers, in poorish heathland soil, either moist or dry. 'Fastigiata', up to 15 m (50 ft) is an erect, Lombardy Poplar-like tree suitable for growing where space is limited. Propagate varieties of *Betula pendula* by grafting which is done in February in a close case.

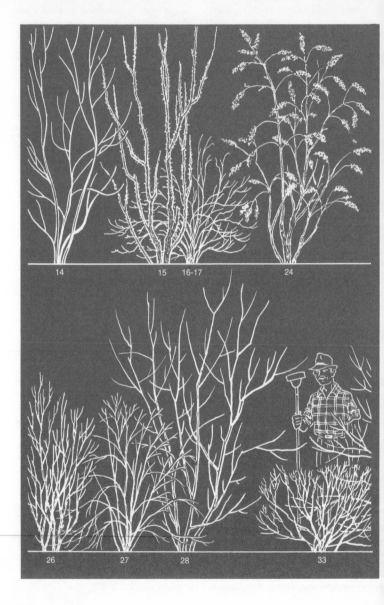

21. Betula pendula 'Tristis'

Height up to 20 m (65 ft). An elegant, tall tree with long pendulous branches and attractive symmetrical habit.

22. Betula pendula 'Youngii'

Height 6-9 m (20–30 ft). The best-known weeping birch which makes a most attractive dome-shaped specimen on a lawn or beside a pool. The pendulous branches are most graceful almost to ground level.

23. Betula pubescens

Common or European
White Birch

Height up to 20 m (65 ft). A native of Europe, including Britain and north Asia. The leaves are more rounded than those of *B. pendula* and it is more tolerant to wet conditions than the Silver Birch. The bark is reddish or brown and on moorlands it may be found often as a bush, rather than a tree, with several stems. Can be raised from seed.

24. Buddleia davidii

Butterfly Bush, Summer Lilac

Height up to 3 m (10 ft). This Chinese species has long been widely grown in gardens and has become naturalised in the British Isles. The large heads of flower from July to September are a great attraction to butterflies. The form *magnifica* is a deep purple-blue and there are also lavender-pink and white varieties. Easy to grow in full sun and in ordinary garden soil. Tolerant of lime. Prune hard in March to obtain strong new flowering shoots. Propagate from hardwood cuttings in autumn.

25. Buddleia globosa

Orange Ball Tree

Height up to 5 m (16 ft). This fast-growing native of Chile and Peru is of erect habit and bears in May and June fragrant ball-like flowers in attractive tapering clusters. The dark green leaves have a wrinkled surface and are semi-evergreen. Prune when necessary after flowering. Propagate from cuttings in June and July—not in cold frame.

26. Callicarpa japonica

Height 1·5 m (5 ft). A neat Japanese shrub with insignificant pink flowers in August but outstanding clusters of violet berries in the autumn. The foliage is also pleasingly rosy-violet tinted in autumn. For pollination purposes plant in pairs or small groups in the spring in ordinary garden soil and in a sheltered sunny position. When the leaves fall in autumn the compact bunches of highly polished berries remain outstandingly on the bare slender stems. Can be raised from seed.

27. Calycanthus floridus

Carolina Allspice

Height up to 2 m (6 ft). A North American shrub with green aromatic leaves felted beneath. The flowers appear in June and July, the fragrance having being likened to that of a brewery, and the wood, when dried, has a camphor-like aroma. Easily grown in a sunny position and in ordinary well-drained garden soil. Often confused with *C. fertilis* which has glossy leaves. Propagate by layering.

28. Caragana arborescens

Pea Tree or Shrub

Height 3–4 m (10–13 ft). A shrub or small tree from Siberia and Manchuria bearing yellow pea-like flowers in May followed by pods, about 5 cm (3 in.) long, containing up to five seeds. Thrives in a sunny position and in poorish soil and being extremely hardy it is useful for exposed positions. Propagate from seed. 'Nana' is an attractive dwarf form suitable for the rock garden and 'Pendula' is a charming weeping form.

29. Carpinus betulus
Hornbeam

Height up to 20 m (65 ft). A native of central Europe, including southern England, and Asia Minor. The leaves are conspicuously toothed and in the autumn they are tinted yellow and russet-brown, but are not as spectacular as the beech with which it is often confused. Mature trees have a deeply fluted trunk and smooth grey beech-like bark. The pendulous fruit with its green bracts is quite distinct from the well-known beech nut. Hornbeam makes an excellent hedge and retains its leaves throughout the winter, like a beech hedge. Easily grown on heavy or chalky soils and a sunny position. Can be grown from seed. There are various forms: 'Pendula' which makes a small tree with wide-spreading drooping branches and the erect 'Fastigiata'.

30. Caryopteris incana, Blue beard

Height up to 1·5 m (5 ft). An attractive small shrub from Japan and eastern China with aromatic grey-green leaves and blue flowers in August and September, and even later. Requires a well-drained soil and a sunny position, or in cold districts the protection of a south-facing wall. In a severe winter the plant may be cut to the ground by frost, but seldom killed and new growth will appear from the base in April. The hybrid C. × clandonensis is hardier and more frequently seen in gardens. Propagate from cuttings in August rooted in a cold frame.

31. Castanea sativa
Sweet Chestnut

Height 20–25 m (65–80 ft). Widespread in southern Europe, including southern England, North Africa and Asia Minor. A handsome tree with deeply fissured grey-brown bark and sharply serrated glossy green leaves up to 20 m (8 in.) long which turn lemon-yellow in autumn. Erect pale greenish-yellow catkins appear in July and August, followed by spiny burrs containing edible nuts (these can be used for propagation). A long-lived tree which thrives on most soils other than shallow chalk.

32. Catalpa bignonioides
Indian Bean Tree

Height 10–15 m (33–50 ft). Although commonly called the Indian Bean Tree, this is a native of the eastern United States. It makes a shapely, round tree bearing conspicuous flower spikes in July and August followed, in a favourable summer, by a heavy crop of slender bean-like seed pods. Requires ample space to be seen as a specimen tree. Likes a well-drained soil and a sunny position, sheltered from summer gales which are liable to damage the large leaves, or break young branches. Propagate from seed.

33. Ceanothus × delilianus

Height 2 m (6 ft). A hybrid of European origin (C. americanus × C. coeruleus) which produces its soft blue flowers throughout the summer. In common with most deciduous ceanothus this likes a well-drained light soil and a sunny position, preferably beside a south- or west-facing wall. Of similar habit 'Gloire de Versailles' has large heads of powder blue flowers and has long been a popular variety and 'Gloire de Plantieres' has deep blue flowers. Not suitable for exposed gardens. Propagate from cuttings in July/August, rooted in cold frame.

34. Cercidiphyllum japonicum

Height 10–15 m (33–50 ft). An attractive Japanese tree with leaves similar to *Cercis siliquastrum* (Judas Tree) but somewhat smaller and opposite, whereas cercis are alternate. The leaves open deep red, soon becoming green and in the autumn have yellow and red tints. The inconspicuous male and female flowers appear on separate trees before the leaves in early spring. A decorative tree for a woodland garden where it can have protection from late spring frosts. Likes a moist soil and is tolerant of lime. Raised from seed sown in Lent.

35. Chaenomeles japonica
Japanese Quince

Height 1 m (3 ft). Widely known as cydonia or 'Japonica' the decorative quinces flower freely in March and April. May be grown in the open border in ordinary garden soil and in a sunny position, or as a wall shrub for any aspect. When trained on a wall pruning should be done immediately after flowering. The edible fruits make good jelly or quince cheese. *Alpina* is a low-growing form with bright orange flowers. Propagate from cuttings rooted in cold frame in July.

36. Chaenomeles speciosa

Height 2 m (6 ft) or more on a wall. An early flowering Chinese shrub bearing fruit suitable for making jelly. There are numerous named varieties of this easily grown shrub in shades of crimson, scarlet, salmon-pink and white. Raised from cuttings as for no. 35.

37. Chaenomeles speciosa
'Nivalis'

Height 2 m (6 ft) or more against a wall. The large flowers are pure white and show up well in March and April

against a red-brick wall. Raised from cuttings as for no. 35.

38. Cladrastis lutea
Yellow-wood

Height 10 m (33 ft) or more. A native of Tennessee and the south-east United States this decorative tree bears its panicles of fragrant flowers in June on well-established trees. The acacia-like leaves turn yellow in the autumn. Likes a loamy soil and a sunny position. Propagate from seed.

39. Clethra alnifolia
Sweet Pepper Bush, White Alder

Height 2 m (6 ft) or more. Of erect habit, this shrub from the eastern United States bears long tapering heads of small white fragrant flowers in August and September, a period when few other shrubs are in flower. Easily grown in a moist, lime-free soil in sun or dappled shade. Associates happily with hypericum and hardy heathers. Raised from seed.

40. Colutea arborescens
Bladder Senna

Height 3 m (10 ft) or more. A vigorous bush from southern Europe with pea-like flowers from June to September followed by large, inflated seed pods. A useful quick-growing shrub for a dry, poor soil and full sun. May be pruned hard back in spring if it encroaches on its neighbours. *C. × media* is similar but with copper-yellow flowers. Raised from cuttings in August.

41. Cornus alba 'Sibirica'
Red-barked Dogwood

Height up to 3 m (10 ft). *Cornus alba*, a native of Siberia, Manchuria and North Korea is remarkable for its colourful autumn leaves and bright red stems in winter of the current year's growth. To obtain a good crop of new growths thin out to ground level in March. There are numerous named forms: 'Sibirica' (Westonbirt Dogwood), illustrated, has brilliant crimson shoots in winter and is most effective beside a pool. Propagate from cuttings rooted outdoors in October.

42. Cornus alba 'Elegantissima'

Height 2–3 m (6–10 ft). A decorative foliage shrub with a broad white margin to the leaves. 'Spaethii' is outstanding with its golden-variegated leaves. Groups of these two can be most effective in a sunny position and moist soil. Cuttings can be rooted outdoors in October.

43. Cornus mas
Cornelian Cherry

Height 3–5 m (10–16 ft). This early-flowering shrub from central and southern Europe bears clusters of small flowers on bare stems in February and March. The fruit is a semi-translucent red berry. The leaves turn reddish purple in autumn. 'Variegata' is outstanding with its white-margined leaves. Easily grown in ordinary garden soil and in a sunny position. Can be layered if new plants are required.

44. Corylopsis willmottiae

Height 2–3 m (6–10 ft). A Chinese shrub of erect habit bearing long racemes of soft yellow fragrant flowers in March and April, on its slender branches before the leaves unfurl. The leaves are often reddish purple in the young stage. Will tolerate lime, but does best in lime-free soil in sun or partial shade. Flowering so early corylopsis, of which there are several charming species, may be damaged by late spring frost, therefore the protection of other shrubs is desirable with a south- or west-facing aspect. Propagate by layering branches.

45. Corylus avellana 'Contorta'
Corkscrew Hazel

Height 3 m (10 ft). The hazel is common in the British Isles, Europe and Asia Minor and its long yellow male catkins, which appear in February before the leaves, are a welcome sight. The leaves turn yellow in the autumn when the pale brown clusters of nuts, much loved by squirrels, ripen. This fast-growing, much branched shrub (6 m) 20 ft or more, likes a well-drained soil in sun or partial shade. Propagate by layering. More curious than beautiful is the slow-growing form 'Contorta' (illustrated) with its much twisted branches.

46. Corylus maxima 'Purpurea'
Purple-leaved Filbert, Hazelnut

Height up to 4·5 m (15 ft). *C. maxima*, the filbert of southern Europe, has larger green leaves and the nuts are longer and larger than those of the hazel. 'Kentish Cob' is a well-known variety bearing large nuts of good flavour. 'Purpurea' has intense purple leaves which make an admirable background for white flowering shrubs, such as *Philadelphus* (Syringa), or white hardy perennials. Easily grown in well-drained soil and seen at its best in a sunny position. Propagate by layering, or by suckers.

47. Cotinus coggygria
Smoke Tree

Height up to 4 m (13 ft). This decorative shrub from southern Europe, also known as *Rhus cotinus*, has an attractive rounded habit and nearly circular leaves, which colour well in autumn.

The silky panicles of flowers are a pleasing feature in July. The variety 'Foliis Purpureis' is outstanding with its light plum-coloured leaves which turn to shades of red in autumn. Easily grown in ordinary well-drained soil and a sunny position. Propagate by August cuttings—not too easy.

48.   Cotoneaster acutifolius

Height 2–3 m (6–10 ft). This species from northern China is one of a large diverse family which includes prostrate forms to tall shrubs, many notable for the brilliant autumn colour of leaves and berries. They are easily grown and like a sunny position. The leaves of *C. acutifolius* take on attractive autumn tints and the reddish berries ripen to black. Raised from seed.

49.   Cotoneaster divaricatus

Height up to 2 m (6 ft). This Chinese shrub of neat growth is one of the best for autumn colour and regular crops of colourful berries. Can be grown as a decorative hedge. Raised from seed.

50.   Cotoneaster horizontalis

Height 60 cm (2 ft). This low-growing Chinese species with herring-bone-like branches spreading to 2 m (6 ft) or more is most decorative for covering a bank or it may be trained against a north- or east-facing wall to a height of about 3 m (10 ft). The small pink flowers appear in June and are a great attraction to bees, hence the unfailing crop of long-lasting berries. Like many other cotoneasters it seeds itself readily, thriving in well-drained soil and in exposed places. Raised from seed.

51.   Cotoneaster multiflorus

Height 2–3 m (6–10 ft). The arching branches of this large shrub from western China are full of hawthorn-like flowers in May followed by large, bright red berries which ripen in August. Makes a graceful specimen shrub. Raised from seed.

52.   Crataegus monogyna
Hawthorn, Thornapple

Height 6–10 m (20–30 ft). The hawthorn or May is common in hedgerows and woods throughout Britain and also widespread in other parts of Europe, North Africa and western Asia. Clusters of white, strongly scented flowers are freely borne in May followed by scarlet or crimson fruit, or haws, each containing a single stone or seed. Propagate from this seed. It makes an impenetrable thorny hedge, commonly called 'Quick'. Thrives in ordinary soil and resistant to spells of drought or waterlogged ground. Does best in full sun but tolerant of partial shade. There are numerous forms: 'Biflora', the Glastonbury Thorn, comes into leaf earlier and sometimes flowers in winter as well as in spring. 'Pendula Rosea' is a graceful weeping shrub bearing pink flowers in May.

53.   Crataegus orientalis

Height 4–6 m (13–20 ft). This Oriental species is almost thornless and distinct with its deeply cut greyish-green leaves. The clusters of white flowers appear in early June and are followed by colourful large berries. It makes a neat small tree attractive both in flower and fruit. Does well in town gardens in a sunny position.

54.   Crataegus oxyacantha

Height up to 6 m (20 ft). From northern and central Europe, uncommon in woodlands in southern England. Similar to the Hawthorn (no. 52) but the leaves are more rounded and it usually produces its white, scented flowers ten days or so earlier than *C. monogyna* and has smaller flower clusters and therefore less berries. It is normally a woodland plant and is a parent of numerous named varieties, probably hybrids with *C. monogyna*. Propagate from seed.

55. Crataegus oxyacantha
'Paul's Scarlet'

Height up to 7 m (23 ft). This makes a shapely shrub which originated in a Hertfordshire (England) garden as a sport. The double, rosy-red flowers are most effective in May and it has been widely planted in gardens. Propagate by grafting on to *Crataegus monogyna* in spring.

56. Crataegus oxyacantha 'Punicea'

Height up to 7 m (23 ft). Bears clusters of single scarlet flowers with a white eye in May. Propagate by grafting on to *Crataegus monogyna* in spring.

57. Crataegus × prunifolia

Height up to 6 m (20 ft). A hybrid of garden origin of compact growth bearing large leaves which are brilliantly coloured in autumn. Clusters of white flowers appear in early June followed by a crop of large round fruit which persists well into winter. A showy shrub for a sunny, open position. Propagate by grafting on to *Crataegus monogyna* in spring.

58. Cytisus × praecox
Warminster Broom

Height 1–2 m (3–6 ft). Of garden origin (*C. multiflorus × C. purgans*) this free-flowering broom is a splendid sight in April and May with its arching branches laden with rich cream-coloured flowers and pleasing grey-green foliage. There is

also a white form 'Albus'. In common with other brooms they like full sun and a well-drained soil, poor rather than rich. Brooms seed themselves freely, but do not come true from seed, and resent disturbance, so should be planted out when quite small. All are best raised from August cuttings or by layering.

59. Cytisus × praecox 'Allgold'

Height 1–2 m (3–6 ft). A shapely shrub of recent introduction with cascading golden-yellow flowers in April and May.

60. Cytisus × praecox 'Hollandia'

Height 1–2 m (3–6 ft). A most attractive variety with a blend of pink and red flowers.

61. Cytisus purpureus
Purple Broom

Height 45 cm (18 in.). A low-growing species from central and southern Europe bearing arching sprays of pinkish-purple flowers in May and June. 'Albus' is a white form, somewhat dwarfer than the type. Requires similar conditions as no. 58. Associates well with hardy heathers and dwarf conifers.

62. Cytisus purpureus 'Incarnatus'

Height 45 cm (18 in.). A free-flowering variety with deeper purple flowers than the type.

63. Daphne mezereum
Mezereum

Height up to 1·5 m (5 ft). A slow-growing shrub from Europe, Asia Minor and Siberia, now rarely found wild in the British Isles, having been transplanted to gardens. The sweetly

49   50   51

58   63   65   66

fragrant flower clusters appear during February and March on bare branches, often topped by a tuft and young leaves. The flowers are followed by clusters of bright red berries which are poisonous, as are the leaves and bark, although birds seem to devour the berries with impunity. The white-flowered form 'Alba' bears yellow fruits and is of more erect habit. Can prove difficult to establish, yet they can be seen flourishing in town gardens in moist soil and in partial shade. Thrives in chalky soil so long as it is moist. Propagate from seed.

64. Davidia involucrata
Pocket-handkerchief Tree, Dove Tree

Height 10–14 m (33–45 ft). A remarkable Chinese tree which bears its conspicuous white, unequal bracts around the flowers in May. The large leaves can be most effective in autumn when they turn scarlet. It requires many years to develop into a flowering specimen, and thrives in any good moist garden soil, in sun or partial shade. The variety *vilmoriniana* has smooth leaves of a somewhat paler green and it may produce flowers at an earlier stage than the type. An admirable specimen tree for a lawn and suitable for town gardens. Propagate from seed.

65. Decaisnea fargesii
Height up to 3 m (10 ft). A Chinese shrub with erect clusters of shoots bearing large pinnate bluish-green leaves up to 1 m (3 ft) long and in June yellowish-green pendulous flowers. The broad bean-like, indigo-blue pods are a remarkable feature of this interesting plant which thrives in moist well-drained soil, in sun or partial shade. Hardy, but liable to damage by late spring frost in exposed gardens. Propagate from seed.

66. Deutzia × magnifica
Height up to 2·5 m (8 ft). A strong-growing hybrid of French origin (*scabra × vilmorinae*) bearing elegant panicles of double white flowers in June and July. Of erect habit, the grey-green leaves are rough to touch. Easily grown in ordinary well-drained garden soil in sun or partial shade. Cut back flowered stems of all deutzias after flowering. Useful for decorative arrangements, but the leaves should first be removed. Propagate all deutzias from cuttings in June/July or October.

67. Deutzia × rosea 'Carminea'
Height up to 1·5 m (5 ft). A hybrid of garden origin (*gracilis × purpurascens*) of compact growth and arching stems bearing clusters of soft pink, bell-shaped flowers in June and July. 'Carminea' has attractive rose-pink flowers and 'Campanulata' has white flowers with pleasing purple calyces.

68. Deutzia scabra 'Plena'
Height up to 3·5 m (11 ft). A tall shrub, with erect branches, from China and Japan, bearing clusters of cup-shaped, white flowers in June and July. 'Plena' has double white flowers suffused rose-purple; 'Codsall Pink', with double rose-purple flowers.

69. Elaeagnus commutata
Silver Berry

Height 2–3 m (6–10 ft). The Silver Berry, also known as *E. argentea*, is a North American shrub with silver-green leaves and in May fragrant, drooping, silvery-white flowers. These are followed by edible, egg-shaped, silvery fruit. A slow-growing plant which thrives in full sun and in sandy or chalky soils. Propagate by layering.

70. Enkianthus campanulatus

Height 2·5 m (8 ft). An erect Japanese shrub bearing dainty, long-lasting, pendulous flowers in May. The leaves, usually in whorls, turn fiery red in autumn. Associates happily with rhododendrons and azaleas in a lime-free, moist soil. Known to Continental gardeners as the Pagoda Bush, due to the whorls of foliage which somewhat resemble a pagoda. Propagate by layering.

71. Euonymus europaeus
Spindle Tree

Height 3–4 m (10–13 ft). A twiggy, green-stemmed shrub common on limestone and chalk lands in Europe, including England. The greenish-white flowers appear in early summer and are followed by most decorative rose-red capsules which open to show the bright orange seeds. The pink- and crimson-tinted autumn foliage with the clusters of fruits, which are poisonous, are outstanding. The hard white wood was used for making spindles and skewers. Unfortunately the spindle tree is a host plant of black aphis, a pest of broad beans. Even more splendid is the Japanese *E. yedoensis*, height up to 6 m (20 ft), which bears larger fruits and larger leaves of more intense autumn colour. Raised from seed or layers.

72. Exochorda racemosa
Pearl Bush

Height 3–4 m (10–13 ft). This large shrub from China needs ample space to display its arching branches of attractive pink-tinted young leaves and clusters of white flowers that appear in April and May. Of graceful habit, this strong-growing shrub thrives in ordinary garden soil, preferably of good depth, and in a sunny position. Useful for decorative arrangements. Raised from seed.

73. Ficus carica
Common Fig

Height 2–3 m (6–10 ft) or more against a wall. Native of western Asia and cultivated in southern England since the 16th century, where it succeeds best against a south-facing wall, or in a cold greenhouse, and in a good loamy soil. In either case the roots should be restricted to an area of about 1 m square (3 ft square) by 1 m (3 ft) deep, by brick or concrete walls, with drainage holes in the bottom. This encourages short growths which are more likely to produce fruit which will ripen. The most suitable variety for cultivation in England is 'Brown Turkey', with brown-green fruits. Grown in a large tub or other container such a fig is both decorative and will produce fruit.

74. Fagus sylvatica
Common or European Beech

Height 20–30 m (65–100 ft). Europe, including southern England, where it is particularly splendid on chalky uplands. In spring the fresh green leaves are a delight and in autumn the wide-spreading, rather pendulous branches with golden-copper leaves are of great beauty. In winter sunshine the smooth silver-grey bark of mature trees is also beautiful. Where beech is planted as a hedge the leaves remain attached throughout the winter thus forming a warm russet-brown screen. The familiar beech nuts or 'masts' are still used for feeding pigs in parts of Europe. Beech timber is hard and much used for making furniture. Propagate from seed, named varieties by grafting. There are numerous named forms of this noble tree.

75. Fagus sylvatica purpurea
Purple Beech

Height 20–30 m (65–100 ft). Makes an imposing specimen tree for a sunny position on a lawn with deep bronze-purple leaves. As it is a large tree and casts a deep shade it is a mistake to plant it near the house, but seen across a spacious lawn it is most effective.

76. Fagus sylvatica heterophylla
Fern-leaved Beech

Height 15–20 m (50–65 ft). An elegant ornamental tree with distinct, narrow, deeply cut leaves. There are several forms of this decorative tree, known as 'Laciniata', 'Asplenifolia' and 'Incisa'.

77. Fagus sylvatica 'Pendula'
Weeping Beech

Height 10–15 m (33–50 ft). A large and imposing tree of varying form usually with long, sweeping branchlets to ground level. There is also a weeping purple beech, 'Purpurea Pendula' which makes an elegant, small umbrella-shaped tree.

78. Fothergilla major

Height up to 3 m (10 ft). A slow-growing shrub from the Allegheny Mountains, U.S.A., related to Witch Hazel (hamamelis), bearing curious flowers in April and May consisting of showy clusters of white stamens, and no petals, with a bottle-brush-like appearance. In autumn the leaves are splendid with shades of orange and crimson. A delightful, trouble-free, yet little-grown shrub which thrives in a light, lime-free, moist soil, with plenty of peat and leaf soil, in sun or dappled shade. Raised from August cuttings.

79. Forsythia × intermedia

Height 3 m (10 ft) or more. A vigorous hybrid (*F. suspensa* × *F. viridissima*) of erect habit with semi-pendulous side growths bearing large, bright yellow

flowers in March and April. There are numerous different forsythias, all extremely hardy and easily grown in ordinary garden soil. They are decorative spring-flowering shrubs for a town garden where they are less likely to suffer bud damage by bullfinches than in a country garden. 'Lynwood', which originated in a garden in Cookstown, Co. Tyrone, Northern Ireland, is remarkably free-flowering and has large, well-formed yellow flowers. Propagate all forsythias by layering.

Forsythia suspensa

Height 2–3 m (6–10 ft). A semi-pendulous Chinese species which requires ample space for its meandering growths. Trained against a wall it will quickly cover a large area, even with a north-facing aspect. Grown in this manner it requires regular pruning after flowering. Sprays cut in January will open in water in a warm room to provide welcome decoration of soft yellow flowers.

Forsythia viridissima

Height 2 m (6 ft). A distinct Chinese shrub which flowers later than most forsythias, bearing its bright yellow flowers in April.

80. Fraxinus excelsior
Ash

Height 15–25 m (50–80 ft) or more. A fast-growing native of Europe, including Britain and Asia Minor. Ash flowers are produced in April or May, before the leaves, and the fruits, or 'keys' form conspicuous, pendulous bunches. Raised from seed. The branches are ash-coloured, hence the common name. The wide-spreading surface roots make it unsuitable for all but the largest gardens, but where space permits the weeping ash, 'Pendula' makes a most imposing tree beside a spacious lawn in any ordinary soil. The whitish, tough wood is widely used for making handles for garden and agricultural tools.

81. Fraxinus ornus
Manna or Flowering Ash

Height 8–10 m (26–33 ft). An attractive tree from southern Europe and Asia Minor bearing an abundance of creamy-white, fragrant flowers in May, followed by green fruits, ripening to brown. Raised from seed. Manna, or a sweet juice, is obtained from the sap.

82. Fuchsia 'Riccartonii'
Hardy Fuchsia

Height 2–2·5 m (6–8 ft). Probably the hardiest crimson and purple fuchsia, flowering freely from July to October, in well-drained soil and in a reasonably sheltered position in sun or partial shade. It forms a most decorative hedge. In the mildest parts of the British Isles and even in less favoured districts it can be grown in this manner so long as it is protected from bitter east winds in the spring. It differs from *F. magellanica*, a South American species, in its deeper crimson calyx and broader sepals, or petals. Propagate from August cuttings.

83. Genista tinctoria
Dyer's Greenweed

Height up to 6 m (2 ft). Native of Europe, including England and Wales, where it is found in rough pasture on heavy soil. Of variable growth ranging from almost prostrate to an erect shrub bearing bright yellow flowers from July to September, in graceful spikes at the ends of the branches. Formerly used to make a yellow dye, or mixed with woad it produces a good green colour. The free-flowering double form 'Plena' is an admirable prostrate plant for the rock garden and 'Royal Gold' makes a neat shrub with rich yellow flowers. These genistas are lime tolerant and thrive in full sun. Propagate from August cuttings.

84. Gleditsia tricanthos
Honey or Sweet Locust

Height 10·15 m (33–50 ft). A North American tree with wide-spreading branches which requires ample space to be seen at its best. The branches and the mature trunk are armed with formidable long thorns. It makes a decorative tree with its light green, fern-like leaves which turn clear yellow in autumn. Small green flowers are borne in July followed by shiny brown seed pods which remain on the tree throughout the winter. Thrives in any ordinary garden soil and is tolerant of town atmosphere. Raised from seed. 'Sunburst', has thornless stems and outstanding bright yellow young leaves. Often listed as *Gleditschia*.

85. Halesia carolina
Snowdrop Tree, Silver-Bell

Height 4–6 m (13–20 ft). A graceful shrub from North America with wide-spreading branches bearing bell-shaped silvery-white flowers in May before the leaves are fully developed. The fruits are pear-shaped, four-winged. Thrives in moist, lime-free soil and in a sunny, reasonably sheltered position. It makes an attractive specimen shrub with its branches almost to ground level. Easily propagated by layering.

86. Hamamelis japonica
Japanese Witch Hazel

Height 3 m (10 ft). An attractive Japanese shrub of upward-spreading form with curiously twisted petals to the welcome flowers that appear in winter on bare branches and are unharmed by frost. The glossy green leaves usually provide a display of rich autumn colour. The witch hazels enjoy a light soil of good depth that retains moisture. They prefer a lime-free soil but can be grown on chalk, so long as it is not shallow, with a liberal addition of peat or leaf soil. Associates well with winter-flowering heathers. Propagate *Hamamelis* by grafting on to seedlings of *H. virginiana* during March.

87. Hamamelis mollis
Chinese Witch Hazel

Height 3 m (10 ft) or more. This Chinese shrub is the most popular of the witch hazels with its cowslip-fragrant clusters of golden yellow flowers from December to March. The fragrance is particularly delightful when sprays are cut and brought into the house. The autumn colour of the leaves can be spectacular.

88. Hibiscus syriacus
Tree or Rose Mallow

Height up to 3 m (10 ft). Of erect growth this decorative shrub from Syria is fairly slow-growing and admirable for the small garden in well-drained soil and in full sun. The shrubby *Hibiscus* is one of the last to show signs of new growth in the spring and it can be late May before the leaves appear. The hollyhock-like flowers are freely produced from July to October. Propagate from July cuttings. There are numerous colourful varieties: 'Blue Bird', single, violet-blue with a darker eye; 'Hamabo', single, blush white with crimson eye; 'Violaceus Plenus', double, wine-purple; 'Snowdrift', single white; 'Woodbridge', single, rich rose-pink with deeper centre. They start to flower when quite young and are among the best of the late-flowering shrubs.

89. Hippophae rhamnoides
Sea Buckthorn

Height 3–6 m (10–20 ft). An extremely hardy shrub or small tree which flourishes mainly in coastal regions of Europe, including Britain. Makes a useful windbreak for seaside gardens in well-drained soil and in sun or partial shade. The catkin-like male and female flowers are borne on separate plants in March and April. When male and female plants are grown together the female bears a crop of dull orange berries during autumn and winter, which are normally untouched by birds. This easily grown shrub makes an impenetrable hedge and will grow equally well inland. Can be raised from seed.

90. Hydrangea macrophylla
Lacecap Hydrangea

Height up to 2 m (6 ft). This name covers a large group of free-flowering plants of Chinese and Japanese origin. The dainty Lacecap varieties have a flat head consisting of a central mass of small fertile flowers surrounded by a ring of large-petalled ray florets. The larger group known as 'Hortensia' (90 a) consist of better-known colourful round-headed varieties, of which there are many named hybrids in shades of pink, deep red, carmine, some of which are blue when grown in acid soil, or when treated with a blueing powder according to the maker's instructions. These strong-growing, decorative shrubs thrive in a soil of good depth that does not dry out and in partial shade, or where grown in full sun a mulch of moist peat or garden compost in the spring will encourage young plants. As the new growth is liable to damage by spring frost they should be grown in a position not exposed to the morning sun. In mild coastal gardens they make exuberant growth. Both types can be cut in the autumn and dried for winter decoration. All hydrangeas are propagated from summer cuttings.

91. Hydrangea macrophylla
'Bouquet Rose'

Height 1 m (3 ft). This hybrid was raised in France by the plant breeder Lemoine and its flowers vary from pink to clear blue depending on the type of soil. It is free-flowering but somewhat weak in the stem.

92. Hydrangea paniculata

Height up to 2·5 m (8 ft). This species from China and Japan bears large pyramidal heads of creamy white flowers in August and September on erect stems. The flower heads become pink-tinted as they mature. To encourage large flower heads and bushy growth cut back the stems in spring almost to the base of the previous year's wood. 'Grandiflora' bears massive heads of sterile florets which last well when cut and dried for winter decoration. 'Praecox' has smaller panicles which appear in July.

93. Hypericum beanii

Height up to 2 m (6 ft). A graceful summer- and autumn-flowering shrub from China, better known as *H. patulum henryi*. The terminal yellow flowers up to 6 cm (2½ in.) across and the deep green leaves make this a most desirable small shrub for a sunny position in well-drained ordinary garden soil. 'Hidcote', a splendid hybrid of uncertain origin, has the largest golden-yellow flowers among the hardy hypericums. Propagate from August cuttings in cold frame.

94. Indigofera gerardiana, Indigo

Height up to 1 m (3 ft) but taller against a wall. This graceful Himalayan shrub has fern-like, grey-green foliage, and pea-like flowers from July to September. Likes a sunny position and enjoys the protection of a south-facing wall. The soil should be well drained and not too rich. Can be grown as a bush in the open border and if cut back by frost will make new shoots from the base. Not hardy enough for exposed districts. Propagate from August cuttings.

95. Juglans regia
Walnut

Height 15–25 m (50–80 ft). A slow-growing native of south-east Europe, Asia Minor and China. Cultivated for centuries in England for its nuts and for timber which is much valued for cabinet making and veneering. Thrives in ordinary well-drained soil and in a sunny position not subject to frost in late spring. 'Laciniata' is a form with deeply cut leaflets, known as the cut-leaved walnut. *Juglans nigra*, the black walnut, is a fast-growing species from the eastern United States with large leaves and deeply furrowed trunk. There are several named varieties, grown as grafted stock, which have been selected for the delicate flavour of the thin-shelled nuts.

96. Kerria japonica

Height up to 2 m (6 ft). A graceful shrub from China and Japan with saucer-shaped golden-yellow flowers in April and May. It is easily grown in ordinary garden soil and in partial shade where it will spread by means of suckers. Old shoots should be thinned out immediately after flowering. 'Pleniflora' (illustrated) is a vigorous double-flowered variety which is taller than the type. 'Variegata' with its dainty creamy-white margined greyish leaves is popular for decorative arrangements.

82   83   85

86   88

164

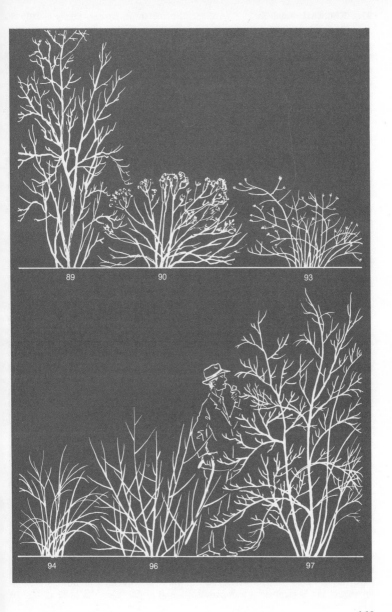

89   90   93

94   96   97

97. Kolkwitzia amabilis
Beauty Bush

Height 2–3 m (6–10 ft). From western China this spring-flowering shrub of elegant appearance bears clusters of urn-shaped flowers at the ends of arching branches. In winter the pale brown peeling bark on the mature stems is quite effective. Easily grown in ordinary garden soil, preferably not too heavy, and in full sun. Propagate from August cuttings.

98. Laburnum × watereri
Golden Rain

Height up to 9 m (30 ft). This tree is a hybrid of *Laburnum alpinum* (the Scotch Laburnum) and *Laburnum anagyroides* (the common species) both indigenous to southern Europe. It flowers in June and will grow in any soil and situation. This and other kinds of laburnum are among the most popular small ornamental trees in Britain. They need no pruning except the removal of any dead wood. As laburnums do not cast very dense shade, it is possible to grow various plants beneath them— those that thrive in dappled shade. If you have the time it is a wise policy to pick off all the dead flower racemes before seed pods form, as the production of vast quantities of seed can weaken a tree. And while on the subject of seed pods, remember that these are poisonous; therefore try to ensure that young children do not eat them. They are quite likely to, as the seeds and pods look like those of garden peas.

99. Lespedeza bicolor
Bush Clover

Height up to 3 m (10 ft). This shrub with pea-like flowers comes from China and Japan and may not be completely hardy in cold areas. The flowers appear in August and September, a lean period

in the shrub border. Stems usually die back in winter, but new shoots are produced in spring. Needs a light soil and warm, sunny aspect. Propagate from seed or by division of rootstock in spring.

100. Ligustrum obtusifolium regelianum

Height 1–2 m (3–6 ft). This Japanese shrub has spreading, almost horizontal branches, making for a graceful habit of growth. The white flowers are freely produced in July and are followed by black berries (100 a). It will grow in a wide range of soils and does not mind partial shade, although growth would probably be better in full sun.

101. Ligustrum ovalifolium
'Aureum'
Golden Privet

Height up to 3 m (10 ft). This bright golden-leaved Japanese shrub is one of the most popular subjects for an ornamental hedge. It stands clipping well and therefore makes a superb formal hedge. The Golden Privet also looks well when grown naturally in a shrub border. It can be grown in any soil in sun or partial shade. *Ligustrum ovalifolium* itself has plain green leaves but is equally suitable for making a formal hedge. Both are excellent in town gardens. Easily propagated from cuttings in late summer or autumn.

102. Ligustrum vulgare
Common Privet

Height up to 4 m (13 ft). This shrub is a native of Europe (including Britain) and North Africa. Can be used as a hedge plant but *Ligustrum ovalifolium* is preferred by most people. The dull white, heavily scented flowers are followed by black berries (102 a). Can be grown in any soil and situation and propagated from cuttings rooted in late summer/autumn. There are various varieties, including the yellow-fruited 'Xanthocarpum'.

103. Liriodendron tulipifera
Tulip Tree

Height 30 m (100 ft). This magnificent North American tree can be grown only in the largest gardens and estates where it makes a superb lawn specimen. It is a spreading tree and will grow fairly quickly given good, deep, loamy soil and a sheltered spot. For most limited space but where height is required there is a narrow-growing variety called 'Pyramidale' or 'Fastigiatum'. The flowers appear during the summer and in autumn the foliage turns a beautiful clear yellow. The Tulip Tree can be raised from seed sown in autumn.

104. Lonicera maackii

Height 3–4·5 m (10–15 ft). This wide-spreading shrub comes from Manchuria and Korea. The fragrant white flowers appear in May and June and are followed by red berries (104 a). The variety 'Podocarpa' is usually considered superior to the species. This *Lonicera* is of easy cultivation: it can be grown in most soils, and fruits best in full sunshine. An excellent plant for the wild garden; probably too large for the average shrub border. Propagate from seed or cuttings in summer.

105. Lonicera syringantha

Height 2–2·5 m (6–8 ft). A vigorous, lax, spreading shrub from China with fragrant flowers in May and June. These are followed by red berries. The variety 'Grandiflora' has larger flowers. Grow in a sunny place, in any soil, and propagate in summer from seed or cuttings.

106. Lonicera tatarica

Height 3 m (10 ft). This shrub is found growing wild from Russia to Turkestan. It also blooms in May and June and has red berries later. Cultivation and propagation as for other loniceras. There are some good varieties of this shrubby honeysuckle: 'Alba' with pure white flowers; *sibirica* with rosy-red blooms; and 'Lutea' described below.

107. Lonicera tatarica 'Lutea'

Height 3 m (10 ft). This shrub is a variety of the species described above and is rather similar except that it has orange berries.

108. Lycium barbarum
Box Thorn

Height 2·5–3 m (8–10 ft). A rather tender shrub from North Africa and Iran, but suitable for maritime areas. Provide a warm sheltered spot and sandy well-drained soil. Can be grown on a wall or trellis. Propagation is by seed or summer cuttings. *Lycium chinense* from China is probably better known and is the species most usually offered in catalogues. It has purple flowers in summer followed by scarlet or orange berries in autumn. Height about the same as above, but stems are spiny and rambling. This species is also much hardier, and has in fact become naturalised in many maritime areas of Britain. Will grow in almost pure sand! Propagate by seed or August-rooted cuttings. It is quick growing.

109. Magnolia obovata

Height 15 m (50 ft) or more. An upright-growing tree from Japan which is quite hardy in Britain. It must, however, be planted in lime-free soil. The leaves are large, up to 45 cm (18 in.)

99   100   102

105   107   108

109   110   111

113   120   122

long, and leathery, and the fragrant flowers which appear in June measure about 20 cm (8 in.) in diameter. The 15–20 cm (6–8 in.) long scarlet fruits are quite attractive. It can be grown from seed and will flower in about 15 years time! Only suitable for large gardens.

110. Magnolia sieboldii

Height 3 m (10 ft). This species comes from Japan and Korea and is suited to smaller gardens. The blooms are fragrant and appear between May and August. They measure about 8–10 cm (3–4 in.) across. It will grow in any ordinary garden soil well enriched with peat or leafmould.

Magnolia kobus

Height 9 m (30 ft). This species is also Japanese and is especially suitable for soils which contain chalk or lime. It does not flower until it is quite large, but then the creamy-white blooms are produced freely in April and May each year. The pink fruits are about 10 cm (4 in.) long. This is a rather slender tree, something like a Lombardy Poplar in shape, and it is fairly quick-growing.

111. Magnolia × soulangeana

Height 3·5–4·5 m (11–15 ft). This is a large hybrid shrub which originated from a cross between *Magnolia denudata* and *Magnolia liliflora*. It is probably the most popular magnolia in Britain, where it is often grown against a wall. Here its branches spread widely. It will also make a good specimen shrub, in a lawn, for example. It blooms between April and June. This magnolia will grow in any ordinary garden soil so long as a good quantity of peat or leafmould is worked in before planting. It blooms when very young and is quite

hardy throughout Britain. The fruits (111 a) are quite attractive. There is a number of equally good varieties to choose from, some with pure white blooms, others white, stained pink or purple.

112. Magnolia × soulangeana
'Lennei'

Height 3·5–4·5 m (11–15 ft). This variety has the same habit of growth and requirements as its parent but the flowers are rose-purple on the outside and white within.

113. Magnolia stellata
Star Magnolia

Height 3 m (10 ft). A slow-growing shrub from Japan. This is the magnolia recommended to those with only small gardens. It is compact in habit and the white flowers are borne in March and April before the leaves. These blooms are fragrant. They are apt to be damaged by frosts, but as the plant produces a great many and they open successively over a long period, the flowers are rarely all destroyed. There is a pink-flowered form called 'Rosea'. Work plenty of peat or leafmould into the soil before planting. Flowering starts when the plant is quite tiny, and continues regularly every year.

114. Malus baccata
Siberian Crab Apple

Height 12–15 m (40–50 ft). An attractive round-headed tree found growing wild from eastern Asia to northern China. Like all the *Malus* discussed here, it is easy to grow, thriving in most soils and situations, including gardens in large towns. It is very hardy even in exposed situations, and especially likes a soil containing lime or chalk. No pruning is needed, except the removal of dead wood when necessary. It makes an excellent lawn specimen. Propagation is by budding or grafting on to apple stocks. As it is a true species it can also be raised from seed. *Malus baccata* is grown for its white flowers which appear in April, and for its bright red autumn fruits. The form called *mandschurica* has larger fruits and this is usually offered by nurserymen rather than the type plant.

Malus 'Golden Hornet'

Height 8 m (26 ft). This is a most attractive hybrid noted for its large bright yellow fruits which remain on the tree until late in the year—usually well after the leaves have fallen in autumn. A good tree for the medium-sized garden. It has white flowers in spring. Otherwise as for no. 114, except it cannot be raised from seed.

115.   Malus floribunda
          Japanese or Showy Crab Apple

Height up to 9 m (30 ft). Originates from Japan. A round-headed tree noted for its pink flowers in May and its autumn fruits (115 a). It is extremely free-flowering, and is a very dense-growing tree. Otherwise as for no. 114.

116.   Malus 'John Downie'

Height 8 m (26 ft). This is a hybrid tree. It bears white flowers in the spring; however, it is not grown for these but for its fruits (116 a), which are surely the finest of all the fruiting Crab Apples. They make excellent crab-apple jelly and when eaten raw have a refreshing flavour. Otherwise as for no. 114, except it cannot be raised from seed.

117.   Malus × purpurea

Height 3·5–4·5 m (11–15 ft). This tree is a hybrid of *Malus atrosanguinea* and

Malus pumila niedzwetzkyana. The beautiful flowers appear in profusion during April/May, and are followed by equally attractive fruits (117 a). The foliage is very ornamental, being a dark purplish green. A tree which can be highly recommended and which is becoming very popular. Otherwise as for no. 114.

Malus sargentii

Height 1·5–2·5 m (5–8 ft). This is a shrub of bushy habit originating from Japan. It is ideal for the smaller garden. In May it covers itself with pure white blooms which have attractive golden anthers. These are followed in autumn by bright red fruits. It is sometimes grown on standard stocks to make a small tree. Otherwise as for no. 114.

118.   Malus × scheideckeri

Height 2–3 m (6–10 ft). The parents of this little hybrid tree were *Malus floribunda* (no. 115) and either *Malus spectabilis* or *prunifolia*. The flowers are borne in great profusion in May and are followed by attractive little yellow fruits (118 a). Otherwise as for no. 114, except it cannot be raised from seed and does not succeed in very shallow chalky soils.

Malus × eleyi

Height 6–9 m (20–30 ft). A superb hybrid crab with rather a wide-spreading habit of growth. The wine-red blooms appear in April and May; the foliage is almost crimson when young but gradually turns coppery red. The red fruits resemble those of a Morello cherry, but are flushed with purple. The parents of this hybrid tree are *Malus atrosanguinea* and *Malus pumila niedzwetzkyana*. Otherwise as for no. 114, except it cannot be raised from seed.

Malus spectabilis

Height up to 9 m (30 ft). A round-headed tree from China. In April and May it produces large clusters of blush flowers opening from attractive deep rose-red buds. These are followed later by bitter yellowish-coloured fruits. Otherwise as for no. 114.

119. Malus halliana

Height 3·5–5·5 m (11–18 ft). Cultivated in China and Japan. The flower buds are carmine and the blooms open pale pink. The small fruits which follow are purplish. Shoots are also purple in colour. The variety 'Parkmanii' has semi-double blooms, opening shell-pink from rose-pink buds. Otherwise as for no. 114.

120. Mespilus germanica
Medlar

Height up to 8 m (26 ft). The Medlar is a native of south-east Europe and Asia Minor, and has become naturalised in England and central Europe. This tree is sometimes spiny and has a somewhat sprawling, often crooked habit of growth—very quaint. It makes an interesting lawn specimen. The large white flowers are borne singly in May and June and are followed by brown edible fruits as shown in the illustration. There is a number of varieties, like Dutch, Nottingham and Royal. The fruits are picked in late October/early November when hard and inedible, and are stored indoors until the green colouring has disappeared and the flesh has become soft. This stage is reached approximately two or three weeks after picking, and the process is known as 'bletting'. The fruits can then be eaten raw or preserved with sugar. Propagation of Medlar varieties is by budding or grafting on to stock of seedling Medlar, Quince or Pear. The type can be raised from seed. Grow the tree in an open

sunny position; most soils are suitable but moist, well-drained loam is preferred. Little pruning is required.

121. Morus nigra
Black Mulberry

Height 6–9 m (20–30 ft). This picturesque tree originates from Western Asia and has been grown for many centuries for its delicious edible fruits. It makes an attractive lawn specimen, and grows well in most soils if well drained and given a sunny situation. This tree usually grows best in the warmer southern half of Britain. It does very well in town gardens. The fruits are picked when they have turned dark, and they are eaten raw. No pruning required, except removal of dead wood. Propagation is from cuttings taken after leaf fall.

122. Paeonia suffruticosa
Moutan or Tree Paeony

Height up to 2 m (6 ft). This is also known as the Tree Paeony, and it originates from China, Tibet and Bhutan. It has many varieties, two of which are shown here. The flowers are either double or semi-double, and 15 cm (6 in.) or more in diameter. Grow in good deep garden soil, acid or alkaline, and protect the young shoots in spring from late frosts. A light covering of bracken, for example, would suffice. It would help also if plants were positioned where they did not receive the early morning sun. They often do well in cold districts, as then shoots emerge later and often escape late frosts. Propagation is by grafting, but is not usually attempted by the amateur gardener. No pruning required.

123. Paulownia tomentosa

Height up to 15 m (50 ft). This largish tree comes from China. It makes a good lawn specimen with its large leaves,

20–25 cm (8–10 in.) wide. Propagation is by seed. No pruning is needed, unless you wish to grow it as a shrub, when the stems should be cut down almost to ground level in March each year. You must start this treatment from the first year of planting. Reduce the resulting shoots to three or four. Very large leaves will be the result and growth will reach about 3–4 m (10–13 ft) in height by the end of the season. No flowers will be produced. It will grow in any soil but likes a sunny position. In some years the flower buds are killed by spring frosts, in which case there will be few if any blooms that year. The flowers open in May/June.

124. Philadelphus coronarius
Mock Orange

Height up to 3–3·5 m (10–11 ft). A popular shrub from south-east Europe and Asia Minor. The very fragrant flowers are produced in June. It will grow in any soil in full sun, and does particularly well in very chalky or limy conditions. For good flowering yearly pruning is required as soon as the blooms have finished. Cut back only the stems that have flowered, to young shoots which are developing lower down. Leave as much young wood as possible as this will produce the blooms in the following year. Propagation is from cuttings taken in November and rooted outdoors.

125. Philadelphus coronarius
'Flore Pleno'

Height 3–3·5 m (10–11 ft). This is a double-flowered form of *Philadelphus coronarius* (no. 124) otherwise the same remarks apply.

Philadelphus hybrids

Height 2–4·5 m (6–15 ft). There are many hybrids of *Philadelphus* and some

of the most popular are as follows: 'Avalanche', small very fragrant blooms; 'Beauclerk', very large flowers with purple staining in centre and good scent; 'Belle Etoile', large, highly fragrant, purple-stained blooms, exceedingly freely produced; 'Bouquet Blanc', a double-flowered variety, free flowering and orange-scented; and 'Virginal', a tall-growing double-flowered variety, very fragrant. Otherwise as for no. 124.

126. Platanus × hispanica
Plane Tree

Height 25–30 m (80–100 ft). This Plane Tree is a hybrid of *Platanus orientalis* and *Platanus occidentalis*, and makes a very handsome specimen in a large garden. It will grow well in a wide range of soils. It is best propagated from cuttings about 30 cm (12 in.) long rooted in a cold frame in October. A very good tree for town gardens.

127. Platanus orientalis
Oriental Plane

Height 25–36 m (80–120 ft). A native of south-eastern Europe and Asia Minor. It makes a huge rounded head of branches, and in a large garden forms an imposing specimen in a lawn, for example. In Britain, where it is a very long-lived tree, it seems to grow exceptionally well—obviously the climate suits it. This Plane can be raised from seed, or cuttings rooted in the autumn. Not fussy as to soil or situation.

128. Populus alba
White Poplar, Aspen

Height up to 30 m (100 ft). An attractive tree which is found wild from Europe to central Asia. It has distinctive smooth grey bark and white woolly shoots, and the undersides of the leaves are also white. There is a variety called

'Pyramidalis' with erect branches, something like the Lombardy Poplar, though not so slender. The White Poplar is an easily-grown tree, not being too fussy about soil or situation. It will thrive in damp soil, but dislikes very dry shallow soils. Said to be good in exposed coastal areas. It is quite easily propagated from cuttings rooted in the open ground in autumn. This tree is not recommended for small gardens because its roots are far-reaching and are liable to damage drains and the foundations of the house. Do not plant less that 15 m (50 ft) away from a building.

129. Populus × berolinensis
Berlin Poplar

Height 18–25 m (60–80 ft). The Berlin Poplar is a hybrid between *Populus laurifolia* and *Populus nigra* 'Italica', the Lombardy Poplar. It is of slender columnar shape and makes a handsome specimen tree. Often used for windbreaks, especially in North America. Otherwise as for no. 128.

130. Populus canescens
Grey Poplar

Height up to 30 m (100 ft). A native of Europe (including England) and western Asia. This is a large round-headed tree, recognised by its yellow-grey bark and attractive leaves which are grey-felted on the undersides. It is a very long-lived species and is said to be one of the best on chalky or limy soils. Otherwise as for no. 128.

131. Populus lasiocarpa
Height up to 18 m (60 ft). This fine Poplar, one of the largest-leaved kinds, is a native of China. The leaves are 15–25 cm (6–10 in.) long and 10–20 cm (4–8 in.) wide. They are bright green and have distinctive red veins. This tree should be planted in a sheltered position for best results, although it is quite hardy. Otherwise as for no. 128.

132. Populus nigra 'Italica'
Lombardy Poplar

Height up to 30 m (100 ft). This tree originates from Italy and is considered by many people to be one of the most impressive fastigiate or columnar trees in cultivation. It is superb when used to form a tall screen or windbreak. Also, of course, it makes a very good avenue. Otherwise as for no. 128.

133. Populus tremula
Aspen or European Poplar

Height up to 15–18 m (50–60 ft). This tree is a native of Europe (including Britain), North Africa and Asia Minor. It is fascinating on account of the scarcely ever ceasing movement of the leaves, which make a restful rustling sound. The male catkins (133 a) grow 5–10 cm (2–4 in.) long and appear in February. They are more conspicuous than the female catkins (133 b). Otherwise as for no. 128.

Populus tremuloides
American or Quaking Aspen Poplar

Height up to 30 m (100 ft) in its native north America, but usually less than half this height in Great Britain. It is very similar in appearance to *Populus tremula*, but can be distinguished from this by its pale yellowish trunk and branches. Otherwise as for no. 128.

134. Potentilla arbuscula
Height 45–60 cm (1½–2 ft). This excellent dwarf shrub comes from the Himalayas and Northern China. It is a close relation of *Potentilla fruticosa*, some varieties of which are described

below. The stems of this *Potentilla* are either upright or procumbent, and from mid-summer to late autumn they bear a succession of large yellow flowers. This long season makes it a popular plant for the shrub or mixed border, where it is usually given a frontal position. It makes a very good companion for *Spiraea bumalda* 'Anthony Waterer' (see page 185). This *Potentilla* succeeds in most garden soils but must have a position in full sun if it is to flower freely. No pruning is required except removal of very old or dead wood, and propagation is by rooting cuttings in a cold frame in August.

135.　Potentilla fruticosa grandiflora
'Jackman's Variety'

Height 1·5 m (5 ft). This shrub has bushy upright growth and a continuous display of large flowers from June to September. It is recommended for shrub or mixed borders and it makes a good informal hedge. Will grow in any soil, but needs full sun; pruning consists of removing old or dead wood, and propagation consists of rooting cuttings in a cold frame during August.

136.　Potentilla fruticosa mandshurica

Height 30 cm (1 ft). This is a low-spreading, semi-prostrate variety with grey leaves and cream flowers from late spring to autumn. Ideal for the front of a border. Otherwise as for no. 135.

137.　Potentilla fruticosa 'Tangerine'

Height 1 m (3 ft). A dense, fairly low-spreading shrub. In cool sunless weather and in the autumn the flowers are coppery red in colour, but in hot summer sunshine the blooms are bright yellow. This was the first of the coppery-coloured potentillas. Otherwise as for no. 135.

138.　Prunus cerasifera 'Pissardii'
Purple-leaved or Cherry Plum

Height 4–5 m (13–16 ft). This is a popular tree on account of its crimson-purple foliage. It is also known as *Prunus cerasifera* 'Atropurpurea'. The flowers appear in the spring. It is seen in many small to medium-sized gardens in both town and country. Tolerant of most soils and situations. This plum is useful for hedge making and it can be clipped when flowering is over. As a tree it needs no pruning, except removal of dead wood. If a badly placed branch needs removing, the best time to do this is between May and July. The cut should be immediately painted with a bituminous tree paint. Propagation is by budding or grafting, and is not usually tackled by the amateur gardener.

139.　Prunus padus
European Bird Cherry

Height 9–12 m (30–40 ft). A native of Europe, including Britain. The sprays of white flowers appear in April and May. This tree is better suited to a wild or woodland garden than to an ordinary ornamental plot, as it is not particularly decorative. There are some superior varieties, such as 'Watereri' with longer racemes, and 'Albertii' which flowers more freely and is more upright in habit. Can be grown in most soils and situations. Remove dead wood when necessary; any other pruning required from May to July. Propagated by budding or grafting.

140.　Prunus 'Shirotae'
Japanese Cherry

Height 4·5 m (15 ft). This cherry is also known as *Prunus serrulata* 'Kojima' and 'Mount Fuji'. The large flowers appear early in the spring on a vigorous horizontally-branched tree. The young

124   125   134   135   136-137

140   141   142   144   145

150 154 160 161

162 164

leaves are bronze-green. An admirable prunus for use as a specimen tree in a lawn or border. Otherwise as for no. 139.

141. Prunus 'Kiku-shidare Sakura'
Japanese Cherry

Height 4·5 m (15 ft). Also known as *Prunus serrulata* 'Rosea' and 'Cheal's Weeping Cherry'. It has a weeping habit of growth and makes a superb specimen in lawn or border. Excellent for the smaller-sized garden. The deep pink double flowers appear in April and May. This is the most popular weeping cherry in Britain. Otherwise as for no. 139.

142. Prunus triloba 'Flore Pleno'

Height 1·5–2 m (5–6 ft). This small prunus comes from China and is especially recommended where space is limited. It makes an excellent wall shrub. The double rosette-shaped flowers are produced freely in early spring. As soon as these blooms are over the shoots which carried them must be cut back hard, almost to their base. This will result in the production of strong new shoots which will then flower freely next spring. Not fussy as to soil.

143. Prunus dulcis
Almond

Height 3–6 m (10–20 ft). A native of the eastern Mediterranean to central Asia. It is a favourite flowering tree in Britain, and it blooms in March/April. The flowers are followed by nuts, the kernels of which are edible. This tree is very prone to a disease called peach leaf curl which causes distorted, red-blistered leaves. This can be controlled by spraying with a copper fungicide or lime sulphur as the buds are swelling in February/March, and again when the

leaves have fallen in autumn. Otherwise as for no. 139.

144. Prunus avium 'Plena'
Double Gean

Height 12 m (40 ft). A native of Europe (including Britain) and western Asia. It is a quick-growing tree and flowers very freely in April. Also, it has good leaf colour in the autumn. Otherwise as for no. 139.

Prunus sargentii
Sargent's Cherry

Height up to 9 m (30 ft). This vigorous, wide-headed tree is suitable only for the larger garden. It originates from Japan, Sakkalin and Korea. The single pink flowers open in March. The young foliage is attractive, being bronze-red. In the autumn the foliage turns to brilliant shades of orange and crimson—making this one of the best trees for autumn colour. Otherwise as for no. 139.

145. Prunus 'Amanogawa'
Japanese Cherry

Height up to 6 m (20 ft). This is a columnar tree, resembling a Lombardy Poplar in shape, and is therefore ideal where space is limited. The flowers are fragrant and appear in April and May and the young foliage is bronze-green. The leaves colour quite well in the autumn. This variety is sometimes listed in catalogues as *Prunus serrulata erecta*. Otherwise as for no. 139.

146. Prunus spinosa
Sloe, Blackthorn

Height 2·5–3 m (8–10 ft). A dense spiny bush from Europe (including Britain), North Africa and western Asia. The shoots are black and the white flowers appear in March and April. These are followed by blue-black edible fruits (146 a) which can be used to make an excellent wine, or jam. It is often found growing wild in the hedgerows of Britain, and it tolerates many kinds of soil and situation. Little pruning is needed. Recommended for a wild garden or perhaps a boundary hedge. There is a much more attractive variety called 'Purpurea' with rich purple leaves and white blooms. It is neater and much more compact in habit.

147.   Prunus subhirtella
Spring or Rosebud Cherry

Height up to 6 m (20 ft). This is a native of Japan and it flowers in early spring. The blooms are of the palest pink. There are numerous varieties of *Prunus subhirtella*, perhaps the best known being 'Autumnalis', the Autumn Cherry, which produces its white flowers intermittently from the autumn through to early spring. Flower arrangers like to cut this for their winter decorations. Unopened buds will soon burst into bloom in a warm room. There are also some good weeping varieties of *Prunus subhirtella* such as 'Pendula Rosea', the Weeping Spring Cherry, with pink flowers in March/April. Otherwise as for no. 139.

148.   Prunus tenella
Dwarf Russian Almond

Height 60–150 cm (2–5 ft). This small shrub is a native of south-east Europe, and is recommended for those with a limited amount of space. The bright pink flowers appear in April. There is a number of varieties such as 'Fire Hill' with bright rose-red flowers; and 'Gesslerana' in bright pink. All of these are ideal for a shrub or mixed border. They are not fussy as to soil and need little pruning except removal of dead

or diseased wood when necessary. Propagation is by budding or grafting.

149.   Pterocarya fraxinifolia
Wing Nut

Height 25–30 m (80–100 ft). This tree comes from the Caucasus and Persia. It is a relation of the Walnut (no. 95), and makes a large wide-spreading specimen, suitable only for large gardens. It has attractive pinnate leaves 20–45 cm (8–18 in.) long. The green flowers, in pendulous catkins, appear in summer. The female catkins grow from 30 to 50 cm. (12 to 20 in.) in length. The males are much shorter. The fruits are winged. The tree grows best in deep moist fertile loam and can be especially recommended for planting alongside lakes and rivers. It is fast growing. Propagation is by seeds, layers and suckers.

150.   Pyracantha coccinea
Firethorn

Height up to 6 m (20 ft). A native of southern Europe and Asia Minor. One of the most popular berrying shrubs grown in Britain. It can either be treated as a free-standing specimen in a shrub or mixed border, or it can be trained flat against a wall or a fence. The shoots should be tied in to horizontal wires or trellis if grown against a wall or fence. It is a thorny evergreen. Pyracanthas will grow in a wide range of soils and situations. They do well on north or east walls. Prune wall specimens after flowering, cutting back any shoots which are too long. Pyracanthas also make good formal or semi-formal hedges. The harder they are clipped the fewer the berries. Hedges are trimmed between May and July. The white flowers appear in June and the berries follow in autumn and last right through the winter if the birds leave them alone. Propagation is by seed, or cuttings rooted in a cold frame in August. The variety 'Lalandei' is equally as popular and has orange-red fruits.

151. Quercus borealis
Red Oak, Northern Red Oak

Height 18–25 m (60–80 ft). This tree is a native of North America and is suitable only for the largest garden. It is noted for its autumn colour—the leaves turn a beautiful shade of red, as can be seen in the illustration. This is a good tree for industrial areas and is very hardy. It requires a lime-free or neutral soil. A good deep rich soil is best. Propagation is from seed.

152. Quercus cerris
Turkey Oak

Height up to 36 m (120 ft). This large species comes from southern Europe and Asia Minor. It is considered the fastest-growing oak in Britain. Grows well in chalky soils provided they are not shallow. A deep fertile soil is recommended. Good for maritime areas. Propagation by seed. The deeply cut leaves are very attractive.

153. Quercus robur
Common Oak

Height 18–30 m (60–100 ft). A native of Europe (including Britain) and Asia Minor. When grown in an open situation this is a large broad-headed tree with rugged trunk and branches. It is very long-lived. Grow it in a good deep fertile soil. Easily raised from the seed or acorns (153 a). Where space is limited and one wishes to grow an oak tree, choose the variety 'Fastigiata' of columnar habit.

154. Rhododendron 'Directeur Moerlands'

Height 120–150 cm (4–5 ft). This is one of the many deciduous hybrid azaleas, botanically classed as rhododendrons. These are placed in various groups according to their origin or parentage, and the variety 'Directeur Moerlands' is one of the Mollis Azaleas. The azaleas in this group are without fragrance and flower in early May. Their foliage takes on gorgeous tints in the autumn, making these dual-purpose garden shrubs. They are ideal for planting in light woodland (pine or oak is ideal) or they are perfectly at home in a shrub or mixed border. They like dappled shade but can be grown in full sun. They must be given a lime-free soil, preferably with plenty of leafmould or peat worked in it before planting. They do not need a very rich soil and light to medium types are best; heavy ground should be lightened with a good quantity of coarse sand or gravel besides leafmould or peat. If possible plant in groups of one variety for best effect— say three or four plants in a group. Keep well watered in dry weather as azaleas like a moist soil. To conserve soil moisture place a layer of peat or leafmould around each plant, about 10 cm (4 in.) deep. No routine pruning is necessary, but it is most important to remove the seed heads, as production of a big crop of seeds can seriously weaken a plant. When twisting off the seed pods, be careful not to damage the buds underneath them. Propagation, from layers, can be carried out at most times of the year.

155. Rhododendron 'Dr Reichenbach'

Height 120–150 cm (4–5 ft). This is also a Mollis Azalea but with gorgeous salmon-orange flowers. It is a very old variety, being raised in 1892. Otherwise as for no. 154.

156. Rhododendron 'General Trauff'

Height 1·5–2 m (5–6 ft). This very old azalea is one of the Ghent Hybrids.

These originated mainly in Belgium, but also in England, between 1830 and 1850. In recent years varieties of this group have been bred in America. The blooms are usually fragrant and appear about the end of May. Otherwise as for no. 154.

157. Rhododendron 'Koster's Brilliant Red'

Height 120–150 cm (4–5 ft). This Mollis Azalea is very well known and has glowing orange-red flowers which make a really good display in the garden. It was raised in 1918. Otherwise as for no. 154.

158. Rhododendron 'Satan'

Height 1·5–2 m (5–6 ft). This variety is in the group known as the Knap Hill Hybrids, which were originally raised in the Knap Hill Nursery in England by Anthony Waterer. They are usually scentless and flower in May. The variety 'Satan' was raised in 1926. Otherwise as for no. 154.

159. Rhododendron luteum

Height 2–3 m (6–10 ft). A native of eastern Europe and Asia Minor. In Britain this is very well known and is often referred to as the common yellow azalea. It blooms in May and the flowers have a very strong fragance. In the autumn the foliage turns to rich shades of orange, crimson and purple. This species is a parent of many hybrids, but is a first-rate garden plant in its own right. Otherwise as for no. 154.

160. Rhododendron schlippenbachii

Height 2–3·5 m (6–11 ft). This rhododendron or azalea comes from Japan and Korea. In Britain, although winter hardy, it is subject to injury by late frosts in the spring. The pink blooms appear in April and May. In autumn the leaves turn to yellow, crimson and orange. The young foliage is flushed purple-red. Otherwise as for no. 154.

161. Rhus typhina 'Laciniata'
Stag's-horn Sumach

Height up to 6 m (20 ft). A native of eastern North America. This large shrub or small tree has deeply cut leaves which take on beautiful autumn colours —orange and yellow. The branches are felty and spread very widely. The plant has a flat-topped appearance. It produces erect conical clusters of green flowers followed by clusters of crimson hairy fruits. This plant will grow in any garden soil and is especially tolerant of town gardens. It makes an attractive lawn specimen. If a smaller specimen is wanted it can be cut back to within a few inches of the ground each spring, and the resultant shoots thinned to three or four. The leaves will be much larger but the stems will reach only about 1·5 m (5 ft) in height. Propagation is by rooted offsets (suckers) or root cuttings. The type plant, *Rhus typhina*, is almost as attractive but the leaves are not deeply cut, although they are pinnate. They turn scarlet or orange in the autumn.

162. Ribes alpinum
Mountain Currant

Height 2–2·5 m (6–8 ft). This is the Mountain Currant from northern Europe (including Britain). The spring flowers are greenish yellow and are produced in erect racemes. The red fruit which follows is not palatable. This shrub has little beauty but grows well in shady places. It is neat and compact in habit, and tolerant of a wide range of soils. It makes a good hedge. The variety 'Aureum' is a smaller shrub whose foliage is bright yellow when young.

163. Ribes odoratum
Buffalo Currant

Height 2–2·5 m (6–8 ft). A native of western North America. This is a much more attractive currant than the preceding species, as it has showy golden-yellow flowers in April and these have a delicious scent of cloves. The berries which follow are black, and the leaves colour well in the autumn. This shrub is thoroughly recommended for shrub or mixed borders and it does well in any ordinary garden soil. Sometimes listed in catalogues as *Ribes aureum*. It will grow in semi-shade or in full sun. Very old wood can be cut out immediately after flowering, otherwise pruning is un-necessary. Propagate from cuttings inserted outdoors in the autumn when the leaves have fallen.

164. Ribes sanguineum
Flowering Currant

Height 2–2·5 m (6–8 ft). This species originates from western North America, and is one of the most popular flowering shrubs in Britain on account of its ease of culture and very early flowering, which is late March/April. It will grow in almost any soil and tolerates semi-shade. Cut out some of the oldest wood each year immediately after flowering. There is a number of excellent varieties including 'Atrorubens', deep crimson; 'King Edward VII', intense crimson (like 164 a); 'Pulborough Scarlet', very deep red; and 'Splendens', rosy crimson.

165. Robinia pseudoacacia
Common or False Acacia

Height 21–25 m (70–80 ft). A native of North America but naturalised in many parts of Europe. This is a most attrac-tive tree with pinnate leaves and scented white flowers in June. Grow in well-drained soil which is not too rich as lush growth should be avoided. This type of growth is very brittle and is easily broken in gales. This tree has naturally rather brittle wood. Propagate from seed. Varieties are propagated by graft-ing on to stocks of *Robinia pseudoacacia*. This tree is especially tolerant of industrial pollution. Some good varieties include 'Bessoniana', smaller growing at 18 m (60 ft), with bright green foliage; 'Pyramidalis', a slender columnar tree, ideal for limited space, up to 14 m (45 ft) high; and 'Frisia', a most striking variety as it has golden-yellow foliage from spring to autumn, and it grows 11 m (35 ft) tall with a similar spread of branches.

166. Salix acutifolia

Height 4–5 m (13–16 ft). This willow is a native of Russia and Turkestan. It is closely related to *Salix daphnoides*, hav-ing similar plum-coloured stems over-laid with a white 'bloom'. The catkins (166 a) appear before the leaves. Growth will be excellent in a moist soil, but very poor in a thin dry soil. The stems show up well in the winter when the leaves have fallen. It can be hard pruned if necessary and is easily propagated from cuttings rooted out of doors.

167. Salix × chrysocoma

Height up to 21 m (70 ft). This willow is considered by many people to be the most beautiful weeping tree in Britain. Consequently it is planted in ordinary small suburban gardens, with the result that in a few years it outgrows them and is then either hacked back or grubbed out altogether. Therefore, only plant this wide-spreading tree if you have a really large garden or estate. It looks its best beside a lake or river, but these are not necessary for its well-being, provided the soil is reasonably moist. The slender shoots are golden-yellow, as can be seen in the accompanying picture. This willow is prone to scab and canker, but young trees can be sprayed with a fungicide containing copper. It may be found listed in some catalogues as *Salix alba* 'Tristis'. It is a hybrid between *Salix alba* 'Vitellina' and *Salix babylonica*. Easily propagated from cuttings out of doors.

168. Salix caprea
Goat Willow

Height 3–8 m (10–26 ft). This shrub or small tree is a native of Europe (including Britain) and north-east Asia. The attractive male catkins shown in the picture are produced in early spring before the leaves. The female form of this willow has silvery catkins. Provide a moist soil if possible and propagate from cuttings rooted outdoors.

169. Salix matsudana 'Tortuosa'
Pekin Willow

Height up to 9 m (30 ft). From China and Korea. This is a most unusual tree as the branches and leaves are very twisted and contorted. But it makes an interesting lawn specimen and of course looks particularly impressive in the winter when the leaves have fallen. Will grow in ordinary soil and is propagated from cuttings rooted out of doors.

Salix purpurea
Purple Osier

Height 3 m (10 ft) or more. A native of Europe (including Britain) and northern and central Asia. An attractive shrub or small tree on account of its purplish shoots. The catkins are borne all along these before the leaves appear. The form 'Pendula' has long weeping branches and when trained as a standard makes a delightful weeping tree, especially suit-

able for small gardens. Otherwise as for no. 168.

170. Salix viminalis
Common Osier

Height 4·5–6 m (15–20 ft). Grows wild in Britain and other parts of Europe. This is a very common shrub on the banks of rivers and lakes and the wood is used for basket making. The catkins appear before the leaves. It likes a moist soil and can be hard pruned to restrict its size if necessary. Propagated from cuttings rooted in the garden.

171. Sambucus canadensis
American or Sweet Elderberry

Height up to 4 m (13 ft). This shrub originates from Canada and the eastern United States. It has pinnate leaves and large heads of white flowers in July. These are followed by purple-black berries. Tolerant of most soils and situations, from sun to semi-shade. An ideal plant for the wild garden. The variety 'Aurea' is much more attractive as it has yellow leaves and red berries. The variety 'Maxima' has enormous flower heads which are almond scented. *Sambucus* are best pruned hard back each spring (almost to ground level if desired) to encourage new shoots and to keep the plants smaller and within bounds. Better-quality blooms will result. Easily propagated from cuttings rooted in the open garden in autumn. Especially good in very chalky soils.

172. Sambucus nigra
Common or European Elder

Height up to 9 m (30 ft). This large shrub or tree is a native of Europe, including Britain. The cream flowers appear in June and are heavily scented. They are followed by heavy bunches of black berries which make a superb wine.

In Britain one often sees people in the country picking baskets of berries for this purpose. The flowers are also sometimes used for making wine. An excellent plant for very chalky soils. The species is not often grown in gardens, however, as it is not considered attractive enough, but it has some good varieties including 'Aurea' with golden-yellow leaves, highly recommended for a foliage border, 3 m (10 ft) tall; and 'Laciniata' with finely divided leaves, about the same height. Otherwise as for no. 171.

173. Sambucus racemosa
Red-berried Elder

Height 2·5–3 m (8–10 ft). This shrub comes from Europe, Asia Minor and northern China. The yellowish-white flowers appear in April and the berries ripen in June and July. Not very free fruiting, unfortunately. The variety 'Plumosa Aurea' is a beautiful shrub with deeply cut golden foliage; it is much slower growing than the type, but makes an eye-catching specimen in a shrub or coloured-foliage border. Otherwise as for no. 171.

174. Sorbaria arborea

Height up to 4·5 m (15 ft). This shrub is a native of China. It is a very large plant and is probably best used as a specimen in a lawn rather than in a shrub border. The flowers appear in July and August. The shoots that have flowered should be cut back in February or March almost to the old wood. Provide a good soil and a position in full sun. Propagation is by seed or rooted offsets.

175. Sorbus aria
Whitebeam Tree

Height 9–15 m (30–50 ft). A native of Europe, including Britain. The large leaves of this tree are felty white underneath and bright green on top. They colour well in the autumn. The white flowers appear in May and are followed by scarlet-red fruits. It will grow in a wide range of soils and does particularly well on chalk. Excellent tree for maritime and industrial areas. Does not mind windswept sites. Propagated from seed.

176. Sorbus aucuparia
Rowan

Height 12–18 m (40–60 ft). This tree is a native of Europe (including Britain) and western Asia. It is very popular in Britain and is extensively planted as a street tree. It makes a very good specimen in the larger private garden. The white flowers open in May and are followed by reddish-orange berries. These are, unfortunately, often quickly stripped by birds in some areas. This *Sorbus* will grow well in a wide range of soils, except very shallow chalky types. Easily propagated from seed. It has some good varieties such as 'Asplenifolia' with deeply cut leaves; 'Fastigiata', a columnar form for those with limited space; and 'Xanthocarpa' with bright yellow fruits.

177. Sorbus intermedia
Swedish Whitebeam

Height up to 12 m (40 ft). A native of northern Europe. The leaves of this tree are covered with grey down underneath. The white flowers appear in May, and orange-red fruits, carried in bunches, follow them. A very good tree for exposed windy situations, and tolerant of a wide range of soils. Propagated from seed.

178. Sorbus koehneana

Height up to 4 m (13 ft). This is a shrubby species from China. It has white flowers in May and white berries. Grows in any good well-drained soil and in full sun. This sorbus can be propagated quite easily from seed. In the autumn the leaves colour up quite well.

179. Sorbus vilmorinii

Height 6 m (20 ft). A shrub or small tree which originated from China. Recommended to those with smaller gardens. The white blooms which appear in spring are followed by rose-red fruits. The foliage is very dainty and ferny. Will grow in any reasonably good garden soil in full sun. Propagate from seed.

180. Spiraea × arguta
Bridal Wreath

Height 2–2·5 m (6–8 ft). This is a reliable shrub, producing its white flowers regularly each year in April and May. The blooms are produced in such quantity that they cover the entire shrub. A good plant for the front of a shrub border where its pendulous shoots are shown to best advantage. Grow in fertile soil and in full sun. Annual pruning is recommended and this involves cutting back the stems which have flowered to young shoots near the base of the plant. Do this immediately after flowering. It is these young shoots which will produce the flowers the following year. Propagation is from cuttings rooted in a cold frame in August.

181. Spiraea henryi

Height 2–3 m (6–10 ft). This is a Chinese shrub which flowers in June. It has an arching habit of growth. Another very good plant for the shrub border. It requires the same conditions and treatment as no. 180.

182. Spiraea japonica

Height 1–1·5 m (3–5 ft). This is a more upright shrub and is a native of Japan. The attractive pink flowers appear in June and July. It is a very popular shrub in Britain. Provide a good deep soil and a sunny position and propagate by division of the plant in autumn or early spring. Pruning each year is recommended and involves cutting back all the stems to ground level in March. Strong shoots will result. A tangled mass of weak growth will result if this pruning is not carried out.

Spiraea bumalda 'Anthony Waterer'

Height 60 cm (2 ft). The flat heads of ruby-carmine flowers of this popular front-of-the-border shrub are produced continuously throughout the summer. Sometimes the leaves are variegated with pink and cream. Otherwise as for no. 182.

183. Spiraea salicifolia
Bridewort

Height 1–2 m (3–6 ft). This shrub is found growing wild from south-east Europe to north-east Asia and it is naturalised in England. Its blooms appear in June and July. The plant spreads quickly by suckers and forms dense thickets of shoots, so lift and divide at regular intervals. In fact it needs the same treatment and conditions as no. 182.

184. Symphoricarpos rivularis
Snowberry

Height 1·5–2 m (5–6 ft). A native of North America. Naturalised in the British Isles. The inconspicuous pink to white flowers are borne in summer but it is the large white berries which follow that are the main attraction. The plant spreads rapidly by suckers and soon forms dense thickets of stems. Propagation is from these suckers. The plant is simply lifted and pulled to pieces. This is an ideal shrub for poor soils and for shaded situations. In Britain it is often used for game cover. This plant is sometimes listed in catalogues as *Symphoricarpos albus laevigatus*.

185. Syringa × chinensis
Rouen Lilac

Height 3 m (10 ft). This lilac is a hybrid of *Syringa persica* and *Syringa vulgaris*. It makes dense bushy growth and the very fragrant lilac-coloured flowers are produced freely in May. It will grow well in a wide range of soils and is especially happy in chalky conditions. Full sun is necessary for good flowering. Little pruning is required, except removal of the weakest wood in spring. Also, cut off the dead flower heads to prevent seed formation as this can weaken the plant. Propagation is from summer cuttings, or layering carried out during the spring.

186. Syringa microphylla

Height 1·5 m (5 ft). This is a Chinese shrub and highly recommended for small gardens. The flowers are very fragrant and appear in June. There is a variety which blooms more freely called 'Superba'. The flowers are rosy pink and appear in May and intermittently until the autumn. Otherwise as for no. 185.

187. Syringa × prestoniae 'Coral'

Height 3 m (10 ft). *Syringa × prestoniae* is a race of hybrid lilacs first raised in Canada by Miss Isabella Preston in 1920, from the species *reflexa* and *villosa*. These lilacs are very hardy and flower later than most, in late May and June. They are very easily grown, need-

ing the same conditions and treatment as no. 185. 'Coral' has coral-coloured flowers.

188. Syringa × prestoniae 'Nocturne'

Height 3 m (10 ft). A purple-flowered form. Otherwise as for nos. 187 and 185.

189. Syringa reflexa

Height up to 4 m (13 ft). This distinctive lilac is a native of China. It has unusual cylindrical pendulous racemes of flowers. These are borne in June; they are not fragrant. The large leaves are, unlike most other syringas, rough to the touch. In Britain this lilac is considered one of the best of the species and it can be highly recommended for the shrub border. It is very free flowering. Otherwise as for no. 185.

190. Syringa vulgaris 'Jacques Callot' Lilac

Height 4·5 m (15 ft). The common lilac, *Syringa vulgaris*, originates from eastern Europe. It is not much grown in gardens, but it has produced a great many varieties, like 'Jacques Callot', which rank among the most popular flowering shrubs in Britain. They have heads of single or double flowers which are very fragrant, and these appear in May or early June. These lilacs make large shrubs, 4·5 m by 4·5 m (15 ft by 15 ft). They can be grown in all kinds of soil and should be given full sun. Chalky soils suit them well. No pruning is necessary, except removal of dead and very weak wood. It is a good idea to remove the dead flower heads to prevent the formation of seed, which could have a weakening effect on the plant. Propagate from cuttings rooted in a cold frame in August, or from layers pegged down in the spring.

191. Syringa vulgaris
'Madame Francisque Morel'

Lilac

Height 4·5 m (15 ft). This is a very old variety of *Syringa vulgaris*, being raised about 1892. It is noted for its very large florets. The habit of growth is upright. Otherwise as for no. 190.

192. Syringa vulgaris
'Marie Legraye'

Lilac

Height 4·5 m (15 ft). This is a popular variety raised in the 1800s. The flowers are white but creamy yellow in bud, and the inflorescences are on the small side. Otherwise as for no. 190.

193. Syringa vulgaris
'Madame Lemoine'

Lilac

Height 4·5 m (15 ft). This variety was raised about 1890 and is an extremely popular double-flowered lilac. The pure white blooms open from creamy-yellow buds. This is highly recommended for the shrub border. Otherwise as for no. 190.

194. Syringa vulgaris 'Primrose'

Lilac

Height 4·5 m (15 ft). A much newer variety raised in about 1949. The small dense panicles of pale primrose-yellow flowers are really most attractive. Otherwise as for no. 190.

195. Syringa vulgaris
'Souvenir de Louis Spaeth'

Lilac

Height 4·5 m (15 ft). This dark-flowered lilac is one of the most popular varieties in Britain, and justifiably so, as it flowers regularly and freely. It is an old variety, being raised about 1883. Highly recommended for gardens. Otherwise as for no. 190.

196. Tamarix pentandra
Tamarisk

Height 3–4·5 m (10–15 ft). A native of south-eastern Europe. This is a large shrub or small tree with delightfully feathery glaucous foliage and feathery rose-pink flowers in August and September. Tamarisk is very tough, thriving near the sea in exposed windy situations. It will grow in a wide range of soils, but does not do well on thin chalky kinds. Best in full sun. It can, of course, be grown inland. If you want to grow this plant as a small shrub about 120 cm (4 ft) tall, prune it almost to ground level in March each year. To grow it as a tree, build up a framework of old wood, but hard-prune the shoots which grow on this in March each year in order to produce good-quality flowers. It is extremely easy to propagate—cuttings should be inserted outdoors in early winter and most, if not all, will form roots. For best effect plant in groups, spacing the plants about 1 m (3 ft) apart each way.

197. Tilia platyphyllos
Broad-leaved or Large-leaved Lime

Height 30–39 m (100–130 ft). This large tree is a native of Europe and is quite a common sight in Britain. Suitable only for parks and the largest gardens and estates, it will grow in any reasonably fertile soil. It bears yellowish-white flowers in July and these are followed by small roundish fruits. The leaves are densely downy underneath. Propagate from seed or by layering.

198. Ulmus glabra
Wych or Scotch Elm

Height 30–38 m (100–126 ft). This is a very large tree from northern Europe. It is also a native of the British Isles, where it has been extensively planted. It has

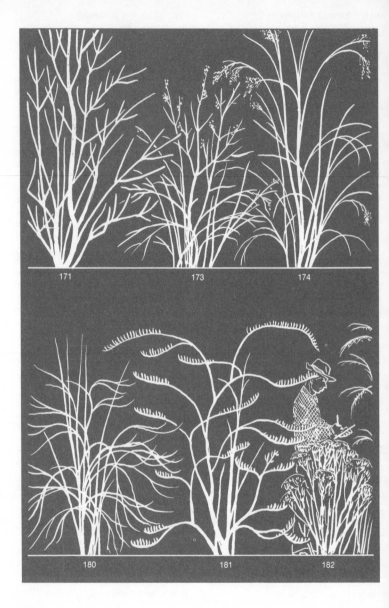

171 173 174

180 181 182

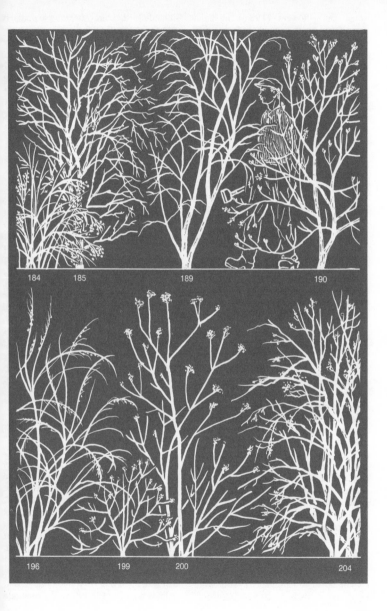

184 185 189 190

196 199 200 204

small pink flowers (198 a) in early spring, and green winged seeds. Incidentally, it is very easily grown from seed. The Wych Elm tolerates exposed situations very well, either inland or near the sea, and can be grown in a wide range of soils. This elm is comparatively susceptible to the Dutch Elm disease which is killing so many elm trees in Britain. This disease is caused by a fungus which is spread by elm-bark beetles. Badly infected trees should be removed and burnt. The odd infected branch should be treated likewise.

Viburnum farreri (fragrans)

Height 3 m (10 ft). This comes from northern China, and produces its pink or white fragrant flowers on erect branches in November and throughout the winter. It does not object to partial shade and is best grown in a sheltered spot. A very popular winter-flowering shrub which can be propagated quite easily by layering the branches.

199. Viburnum carlesii

Height 1·5–2·5 m (5–8 ft). This shrub is a native of Korea. It is extremely popular in Britain. In April and May clusters of pure white flowers appear on this compact, rounded bush. The blooms have a very strong sweet fragrance. The berries which follow are jet-black. In cold areas plant this shrub in a position where it receives slight protection and shade on the eastern side, to save the buds from damage by late spring frosts. Grows well in any good garden soil, including chalky types. Propagate from cuttings rooted in a close frame in July.

200. Viburnum lantana

Wayfaring Tree

Height up to 4·5 m. (15 ft). This large vigorous shrub is a native of Europe,

including Britain. It is particularly abundant on the chalk downs in the south of the country. The creamy-white flowers appear in May and June and these are followed by red fruits which eventually turn black. The foliage usually turns crimson in the autumn. This is a good plant for a wild or natural garden. Propagate from cuttings rooted in a close frame in July.

201. Viburnum opulus 'Sterile'

Snowball Tree, European
Cranberry Bush

Height 3–3·5 m (10–11 ft). *Viburnum opulus* is a native of Europe, including Britain. The variety 'Sterile' is a very popular viburnum on account of the many balls of white flowers which are produced in June and July. The flowers are all sterile, hence the name. The foliage colours very well in the autumn. This shrub grows particularly well in moist soil and does not mind partial shade. The type plant, *Viburnum opulus*, is also well worth growing—it bears flattened heads of blooms in June and July and these are followed by striking red fruits and brilliant autumn colour. Propagate from cuttings rooted in July in a close frame.

202. Viburnum tomentosum 'Mariesii'

Japanese Snowball

Height 2–3 m (6–10 ft). *Viburnum tomentosum* is a native of China and Japan. The variety 'Mariesii' is to be preferred as a garden plant. In June the bush carries so many white flowers that it looks as though it is covered with snow. The branches are horizontal so it makes quite a wide-spreading specimen. It makes a good lawn shrub. This plant will grow in any reasonably good garden soil, including very chalky ones, and it likes a position in full sun. Propagate from cuttings rooted in a close frame in July.

203. Weigela florida

Height 2–2·5 m (6–8 ft). This shrub is a native of northern China, Japan, Korea and Manchuria. In May and June it produces funnel-shaped pink flowers. After flowering it is important to prune it: cut back the stems which have flowered to young shoots which are growing near the base. This will result in prolific and regular flower production. This shrub should be grown in moderately rich soil and in full sun. It is excellent for town gardens and in Britain is a very popular flowering shrub. Propagate from cuttings rooted out of doors in November.

204. Weigela 'Bristol Ruby'

Height 2 m (6 ft). This is a hybrid with gorgeous ruby-red flowers in May and June. It is very free flowering. Cultivation and conditions required as for no. 203.

205. Weigela florida 'Variegata'

Height 2 m (6 ft). This is one of the best variegated-leaved shrubs for planting either in a shrub border or a coloured-foliage border. Also recommended is the purple-leaved form of *Weigela florida* called 'Foliis Purpureis'. Both have pink flowers. Cultivation and conditions required as for no. 203.

206. Weigela 'Mont Blanc'

Height 2 m (6 ft). This is the best white hybrid *Weigela*. It is very vigorous and has large flowers which are fragrant. Cultivation and conditions required as for no. 203.

207. Weigela middendorffiana

Height 60–120 cm (2–4 ft). A native of northern China, Manchuria and Japan, producing in April and May large yellow flowers. Best in a sheltered position, partially shaded. Otherwise as for no. 203.

SHRUB ROSES

208. Rosa × alba 'Maiden's Blush'

Height 1·5 m (5 ft). This variety is an old-fashioned shrub rose originating from the hybrid *Rosa alba*. There are really two varieties: 'Great Maiden's Blush', and 'Small Maiden's Blush' which is practically the same but slightly lower growing. They originated prior to the 15th century. The flowering period is mid-summer, and the blooms are very fragrant. This type of rose is best grown in a border with other shrubs, or in a mixed border. It is tolerant of a wide range of soils but is best given a position in full sun. There is no need to do much pruning of this rose. All that is necessary is the removal of dead wood; also, occasionally cut out

some of the very old wood. This is best done in March. A mulch of well-rotted manure or garden compost in the spring would be appreciated. This rose remains comparatively free from pests and diseases. It can be propagated from cuttings of well-ripened young shoots inserted in the open ground in the autumn. The cuttings should be about 30 cm (12 in.) long and inserted to about two-thirds of their length. They take about a year to form a good root system. A hormone rooting powder will greatly assist root formation.

209. Rosa carolina

Height 60–90 cm (2–3 ft). This is a species which originates from the north-east United States. The rose-pink single flowers, about 5 cm (2 in.) across, appear in June. The stems are very bristly when young. There is a double-flowered form called *Rosa carolina* 'Plena' and the colour of this is shell-pink to pale salmon-pink. It grows only about 60 cm (2 ft) high. Can be raised from seed or cuttings. Otherwise as for no. 208.

210. Rosa foetida 'Persiana'
Persian Yellow Rose

Height 1·5 m (5 ft). This old rose, introduced in 1838 from western Asia, has richly scented, fully double, brilliant yellow blooms in mid-summer. This free-flowering shrub was crossed with hybrid perpetual roses, giving us the pernetiana race, eventually merged into the hybrid teas. These were the first yellow roses of modern appearance. The Persian Yellow is still worth growing in gardens in its own right. Otherwise as for no. 208.

211. Rosa helenae

Height 3–6 m (10–20 ft). This rose is a native of China. It is a very vigorous climber with stout thorns and reddish young shoots. The white flowers are 2–3 cm ($\frac{3}{4}$–1 in.) across and they are fragrant. They appear in June and July, and are followed by small red hips in the autumn (211 a). This rose is excellent for growing over old trees, hedges and so on. Can be raised from cuttings. Otherwise as for no. 208.

212. Rosa moyesii

Height 3·5 m (11 ft). A splendid shrub originating from western China. The single blood-red flowers, 4–7 cm ($1\frac{1}{2}$–$2\frac{3}{4}$ in.) across, appear in mid-summer and look superb against the lacy foliage. In autumn the plant makes another spectacular display with its vermilion-red hips (212 a). There is a good variety called 'Geranium', similar in the colour of its flowers and hips, but a little shorter and more compact in habit of growth. Otherwise as for no. 208.

213. Rosa 'Nevada'

Height 2 m (6 ft). This is classed as a modern shrub rose, being introduced in 1927. It is said to be the result of a cross between the hybrid tea 'La Giralda' and *Rosa moyesii*. It is vigorous and produces its large single creamy-white flowers in profusion in late May and June. There is another flush of blooms in late summer. This rose is well worth a place in any shrub border. Otherwise as for no. 208.

214. Rosa omeiensis pteracantha
Mount Omei Rose

Height 2·5 m (8 ft). This shrub is a native of western China. In mid-summer it produces masses of small white scented flowers—these have only four petals instead of the usual five. The flowers are followed by showy orange-red hips. The thorns are extremely attractive, being very wide and translucent red. They are most impressive on the young shoots. The ferny foliage adds to the charm of this shrub rose. Otherwise as for no. 208.

215. Rosa rubrifolia

Height 1·5 m (5 ft). A first-class shrub rose which originates from Europe. First, the leaves are soft greyish green with a purplish sheen, and the bark is reddish brown. Second, masses of bright pink blooms are produced in mid-summer. And third, reddish-brown hips are produced in the autumn. So from spring until well into autumn this rose has colour and interest to offer. It should be grown in every garden. Incidentally, the stems are almost thornless. Otherwise as for no. 208.

216. Rosa rugosa
Ramanas Rose

Height 1·5–2·5 m (5–8 ft). This is a native of northern China, Korea and Japan. It is a very prickly species and that is probably why it is so often recommended as a hedging plant! The solitary flowers are fragrant and appear in June and July. *Rosa rugosa* is a good fruiting species and it has quite large orange-red hips which ripen in early autumn. The leaves turn to a pleasing shade of yellow in the autumn. This species has quite a few varieties and forms, all of which can be thoroughly recommended for garden decoration. The type can be raised from seed or cuttings. Otherwise as for no. 208.

217. Rosa rugosa 'Frau Dagmar Hastrup'

Height 1·5 m (5 ft). This is a superb variety of the above species and should be grown in every shrub or mixed border. The large clear pale pink blooms are produced throughout the summer from attractive pointed buds. In the autumn there is a profusion of large red hips (217 a). Otherwise as for no. 208.

218. Rosa rugosa 'Stella Polaris'

Height 120 cm (4 ft). This is a very old variety, raised about 1890. It has large silvery-white single flowers with a boss of yellow stamens, and they are produced throughout the summer. A vigorous rose. 'Stella Polaris' is not well known in Britain and it is doubtful whether it is even obtainable. However, a very good substitute would be *Rosa rugosa* 'Alba' which is taller at 2 m (6 ft). It produces a heavy crop of showy orange-red hips which contrast well with the late blooms. Otherwise as for no. 208.

219. Rosa blanda
Meadow Rose

Height 120–180 cm (4–6 ft). This species is a native of eastern and central North America. The stems have very few prickles. It is an early-flowering rose, the rose-pink blooms appearing in May and June. They measure about 5 cm (2 in.) across. These are followed by red fruits in the autumn, when the foliage turns yellow. This rose is not very well known in Britain. It can be raised from seed or cuttings. Otherwise as for no. 208.

220. Rosa gallica
French Rose

Height 60–90 cm (2–3 ft). This species is found wild from southern Europe to western Asia. It is a very prickly shrub with single pink flowers in June and brick-red hips in the autumn. These are shown in the accompanying illustration. The species is not often grown in gardens, but it is the parent of many old garden roses which are still well worth growing. *Rosa gallica* 'Versicolor', also known as 'Rosa Mundi', is a popular one—its crimson flowers are splashed and striped with blush white. Otherwise as for no. 208.

221. Rosa hugonis

Height 2 m (6 ft). A native of Central China. This species is very popular with gardeners in Britain. It is very early flowering, producing its single yellow flowers in May and June. The small round deep red hips ripen in July and August but are not very showy. The fern-like foliage is most attractive, however. An invaluable rose for providing some early colour in the shrub border.

Otherwise as for no. 208. It can be raised from seed.

222. Rosa multiflora

Height 3·5 m (11 ft). A climbing species from Japan and Korea. It is usually thornless, or almost thornless, and forms quite a dense thicket of growth. It makes quite a good hedge. Small white flowers are produced in June and July and these are followed by tiny red hips. The flowers are well scented. This rose could be used for covering tree stumps and the like. It is not too well known in Britain. Otherwise as for no. 208. It can be raised from seed or cuttings.

223. Rosa pendulina

Height 1–1·5 m (3–5 ft). This species is a native of central and southern Europe and is quite distinctive on account of its smooth cane-like reddish young stems. The flowers are rose-purple and appear in June. The flask-shaped fruits, which are illustrated, are quite showy and are about 2·5 cm (1 in.) long. There is a very good double-flowered form called *Rosa pendulina* 'Flore Pleno', which has colourful young foliage as well as good autumn colour. Otherwise as for no. 208.

224. Rosa spinosissima

Height 1 m (3 ft). A native of Europe (including Britain) and western Asia. In May this species produces deliciously scented single blooms in creamy white and these are followed by shiny black hips as shown in the accompanying illustration. It grows best in a sandy soil or other light garden soil. It can in fact be grown in most soils provided they are not too wet. This is a very prickly species which forms thickets of stems, and it spreads quickly by underground runners. Propagate by removing rooted runners or by stem cuttings. Otherwise as for no. 208.

225. Rosa spinosissima
'Frühlingsgold'

Height 2·5 m (8 ft). This superb hybrid was raised by Wilhelm Kordes in Germany. In May and June the arching branches bear huge yellow blooms all along their length. These are beautifully scented. The stems are best given some form of support, such as a stout post, to which they can be tied in. Otherwise as for nos. 224 and 208.

226. Rosa spinosissima
'Frühlingsmorgen'

Height 2 m (6 ft). Another of Wilhelm Kordes' superb *spinosissima* hybrids, this time with huge clear pink blooms. It is recurrent flowering and a good crop of blooms is produced in September. The flowers are beautifully fragrant. Maroon-red hips are produced in the autumn and these are also illustrated (226 a). The stems are best tied in to a stout post. Otherwise as for nos. 224 and 208.

HYBRID TEA AND FLORIBUNDA ROSES

227. 'Orangeade'

Floribunda

Height 75 cm (2½ ft). A superb rose with brilliant orange blooms. Introduced in 1959 and still very popular. The floribundas are first-class roses for garden display as they produce their blooms in large clusters throughout the summer. The best way to grow them is to mass them in formal beds and borders—a bed of one variety can look most striking or, of course, varieties can be mixed. The floribundas can also look effective in a mixed border (containing a mixture of different plants such as shrubs, herbaceous perennials and bulbs). Indeed, this is a popular way of growing them in the modern small garden. They will grow in a very wide range of soils and do particularly well on clay or other heavy types if well drained. They will not grow so well on very chalky soils, especially thin chalky soils, as in these they are unable to obtain sufficient iron and therefore the leaves will be sickly yellow and growth generally poor. This trouble, known as lime-induced chlorosis, can be cured by watering the ground around the plants with an iron sequestrol according to the manufacturer's instructions. Floribundas like a rich soil, so dig in plenty of well-rotted manure or garden compost before planting, and work bonemeal into the surface at the rate of 120 gm (4 oz) per square metre (square yard). Plant in autumn or winter, 45–60 cm (18–24 in.) apart each way. These roses must be given a position in full sun.

For really good flower production feed your roses with a proprietary rose fertiliser in spring and summer according to the maker's instructions. Also, if desired, mulch with rotted manure or compost. Annual pruning must also be practised in March. Cut out dead and diseased wood and very weak stems, and shorten the remainder to about half their length for the strong ones, and to about one-third for weaker ones. Cut just above an outward-facing bud each time. It is an unfortunate fact that these roses are attacked by diseases to a greater or lesser extent according to variety and the area in which they are grown. Roses in industrial areas with atmospheric pollution are not usually badly affected. Black spot and mildew are the commonest diseases, the former appearing as black spots on the leaves which

gradually coalesce, and the latter as white powder on leaves and shoot tips. Apply a fungicide at two-weekly intervals from mid-April to late September—for example one containing captan, maneb, thiram or dinocap—to keep these diseases well under control. Or use the new systemic fungicide which circulates in the sap stream of the plant and therefore is not washed off the leaves by rain. Far fewer applications of this are necessary. Greenflies, the most common pests of roses, can be controlled by spraying with a systemic insecticide containing menazon, formothion or dimethoate at regular intervals between May and September. Keep removing dead blooms to encourage flower production, and keep the plants well watered in dry weather. Propagation is by budding in July, using rootstocks of *Rosa canina, Rosa laxa* or *Rosa multiflora*. Sometimes cuttings can be rooted and this method of propagation would probably be found easier and less troublesome by the amateur.

228. 'Piccadilly'
Hybrid Tea

Height 75 cm (2½ ft). A 1960 introduction and one of the famous bicolour roses. Foliage reasonably disease resistant. Hybrid teas are best grown in formal beds and borders, either one variety per bed or mixed. Blooms are more formal than those of floribundas, are borne singly or in smaller clusters, and are produced throughout summer. Otherwise as for no. 227.

229. 'Polka'
Floribunda

Height 75 cm (2½ ft). This is an attractive small-flowered floribunda introduced in 1960, in a pleasing shade of salmon-pink, but unfortunately it is not

208   213

216   221

230   233   238   241

268   269

very well known in Britain. A good substitute would be 'Pernille Poulsen' which is extremely free flowering. Otherwise as for no. 227.

230. 'Queen Elizabeth'
Floribunda—Hybrid Tea Type

Height up to 2 m (6 ft). A very famous rose introduced in 1955. The clear pink flowers are medium-sized and are slightly fragrant. They are produced very freely. As well as being an excellent tall bedding rose, 'Queen Elizabeth' is also highly recommended as a hedging plant. It was awarded the President's International Trophy by the Royal National Rose Society (R.N.R.S.) in 1955. Cultivation as for no. 227.

231. 'Red Queen'
Hybrid Tea

Height 105 cm (3½ ft). A huge red rose, excellent for exhibition as well as garden decoration, which was raised by Wilhelm Kordes and introduced in 1968. The tall upright plant gives good long stems for cutting. Otherwise as for nos. 227 and 228.

232. 'Iceberg'
Floribunda

Height 105 cm (3½ ft). Another variety raised by Wilhelm Kordes and introduced in 1958. The result of a cross between 'Robin Hood' and 'Virgo', it is the best white floribunda so far raised and deservedly enjoys immense popularity. The flowers are pure white when fully open but there is a slight pink tinge in the bud stage. The blooms are fragrant and are borne freely on a very vigorous plant. Flowers well into the winter. Otherwise as for no. 227.

233. 'Super Star'
Hybrid Tea

Height 1 m (3 ft). Raised by Tantau of France, this famous rose appeared in 1960 and was the first with this particular colour—pure light vermilion. The flowers are very freely produced, are fragrant and are carried on a vigorous plant. It has plenty of healthy glossy dark foliage. This universal favourite makes an eye-catching splash of colour in a bed. It was awarded the President's International Trophy by the R.N.R.S. in 1960. Otherwise as for nos. 227 and 228.

234. 'Sutter's Gold'
Hybrid Tea

Height 1 m (3 ft). This is a well-known rose introduced in 1950. The yellow blooms are flushed with pink and are borne very freely. They have a very sweet scent, and appear quite early in the season. The foliage is usually quite healthy. Otherwise as for nos. 227 and 228.

235. 'Uncle Walter'
Hybrid Tea

Height 120–150 cm (4–5 ft). This is a very vigorous strong-growing rose introduced in 1963. Raised by Sam McGredy, it was the result of a cross between 'Brilliant' and 'Heidelberg'. The blooms are produced very freely and are of classical hybrid-tea shape—ideally suited to exhibition work. The rich red colour does not fade with age, and does not 'blue'. Otherwise as for nos. 227 and 228.

236. 'Western Sun'
Hybrid Tea

Height 1 m (3 ft). This was raised in Denmark by D. Poulsen and introduced in 1965. The deep yellow blooms have good colour stability. It is quite resistant to bad weather and diseases, and has light green matt foliage. Otherwise as for nos. 227 and 228.

237. 'Whisky Mac'
Hybrid Tea

Height 1 m (3 ft). Raised by Tantau of France and introduced in 1967. This rose is extremely popular on account of its unusual colour which can best be described as amber. It is very free flowering and excellent for cutting. It is especially liked by flower arrangers. The blooms are reasonably rain resistant; the foliage is inclined to suffer from mildew. Otherwise as for nos. 227 and 228.

238. 'Allgold'
Floribunda

Height 75 cm (2½ ft). Introduced in 1956 by Le Grice, this rose should be in every garden. It is the best of the yellow floribundas. The slightly scented blooms in large trusses are rain resistant and the colour is remarkably stable. It is an exceedingly free-flowering rose and has a compact bushy habit of growth. Otherwise as for no. 227.

239. 'Chinatown'
Floribunda

Height 120–150 cm (4–5 ft). This very tall vigorous floribunda was introduced in 1963, having been raised by Poulsen. The yellow flowers are 10 cm (4 in.) across when fully opened and are carried in small clusters. They are very slightly fragrant and are produced very freely indeed. The lush foliage is light green. This rose can be used for bedding or as a shrub in a mixed border. Otherwise as for no. 227.

240. 'City of Belfast'
Floribunda

Height 75 cm (2½ ft). This was introduced in 1968 by McGredy, and has been given the R.N.R.S. President's International Trophy. It is a superb bedder as it blooms continuously throughout the summer and the flowers are an eye-catching bright orange-scarlet, the colour being stable. Disease resistant. Otherwise as for no. 227.

241. 'Cricri'
Miniature

Height 30 cm (12 in.). A Meilland rose introduced in 1958. The little salmon-pink blooms are freely produced on a small compact bushy plant. The miniature roses are ideal for edging beds and borders, and for growing in containers such as garden tubs and window boxes. Owners of very small gardens will especially appreciate them. Otherwise as for no. 227.

242. 'Fragrant Cloud'
Hybrid Tea

Height 1 m (3 ft). Raised by Tantau and introduced in 1964. This is one of the most beautifully fragrant modern roses —it has an exceedingly strong fruity scent. The large flowers are very shapely and are freely produced. The strong growth is quite resistant to disease. A good all-round bedding rose. Otherwise as for nos. 227 and 228.

243. 'Isis'
Floribunda

Height 75 cm (2½ ft). This is to be introduced by John Mattock of Oxford in 1973 and could well be a serious rival to 'Iceberg'. It carries clusters of pure white blooms which are delicately tinged with green before they are fully

open. Good to see a new white floribunda. Otherwise as for no. 227.

244. 'Elizabeth of Glamis'
Floribunda

Height 75 cm (2½ ft). Raised by
McGredy and introduced in 1964, this
rose has won the R.N.R.S. President's
International Trophy, and the Clay Cup
for fragrance. It has, of course, been
named after Her Majesty The Queen
Mother. The foliage is generally quite
healthy. Otherwise as for no. 227.

245. 'Europeana'
Floribunda

Height 75 cm (2½ ft). Introduced in
1963; raised by De Ruiter. This rose has
deep crimson flowers which are very full
and rosette shaped and carried in
medium-sized trusses. They are only
slightly fragrant but produced very freely
on a vigorous bushy plant. An ideal bedding rose. The foliage is attractive also, as
it is dark red. Otherwise as for no. 227.

246. 'Farandole'
Floribunda

Height 75 cm (2½ ft). A Meilland rose
introduced in 1959. A moderately
vigorous, very free-flowering variety
with large trusses of well-formed semi-
double light vermilion blooms. Not
popular nowadays but a good rose
nevertheless. Otherwise as for no. 227.

247. 'Grand'mère Jenny'
Hybrid Tea

Height 1 m (3 ft). Another Meilland
variety, introduced in 1950. The large,
full, well-formed, slightly fragrant
flowers are light yellow flushed with deep
pink, and are produced very freely on a
vigorous upright bush. Otherwise as for
nos. 227 and 228.

248. 'Hakuun'
Floribunda

Height 60 cm (2 ft). This most attractive
Danish rose was introduced by Poulsen
in 1966 and is currently available in
Britain from R. Harkness and Co. Ltd.,
of Hitchin, Herts. The semi-double
white to cream flowers are borne in
great profusion on a vigorous short
busy plant. Otherwise as for no. 227.

249. 'Alexander'
Hybrid Tea

Height 1 m (3 ft) or more. A Harkness
rose introduced in 1972. This is really
sensational as the colour is a brilliant
vermilion-red which is held well. The
plant is strong growing and the foliage
disease resistant. The blooms stand
quite a lot of bad weather. Suitable for
bedding or as a hedge. Otherwise as for
nos. 227 and 228.

250. 'Intermezzo'
Hybrid Tea

Height 75 cm (2½ ft). This rose was
introduced in 1963 and was raised in
Spain by Dot. It is a free-flowering lilac-
coloured variety of below average
height, but of bushy habit. This colour is
very popular among flower arrangers
nowadays. Other good varieties in this
colour include 'Blue Moon' (raised by
Tantau of Germany, introduced 1964),
fragrant, 105 cm (3½ ft); and Godfrey
Winn (raised by Dot of Spain,
introduced 1968), very strong scent, 1
m (3 ft). Otherwise as for nos. 227 and
228.

251. 'Jan Spek'
Floribunda

Height 1 m (3 ft). Raised by McGredy
and introduced in 1966. This is a good
deep yellow bedding rose with flowers of

high quality. These are produced very freely on a compact bush. Otherwise as for no. 227.

252. 'Korona'
Floribunda

Height 120 cm (4 ft). Raised by Wilhelm Kordes of Germany and introduced in 1953. This is a cheerful bedding rose in bright orange-scarlet, fading to deep salmon. The slightly fragrant flowers are borne freely and continuously in large trusses. It is very vigorous in habit and makes quite a large plant. Can be used for bedding or for planting in a mixed border. Like all of Kordes' varieties it is highly recommended for garden decoration. Also good for cutting. Otherwise as for no. 227.

253. 'Perfecta'
Hybrid Tea

Height 1 m (3 ft). Another Kordes' variety, introduced in 1957. The flowers are very large, very full and of perfect shape. They are also fragrant and freely produced. The bush is vigorous and bears plenty of deep green glossy foliage. A good rose for cutting and for bedding. The blooms will not put up with too much rain, unfortunately. Winner of R.N.R.S. President's International Trophy. Otherwise as for nos. 227 and 228.

254. 'Colour Wonder'
Hybrid Tea

Height 1 m (3 ft). This is a Kordes' variety which appeared in 1964. It is an excellent bicolor rose in orange and yellow. The blooms are very full and shapely. An excellent bedding rose. Otherwise as for nos. 227 and 228.

255. 'Champs Elysées'
Hybrid Tea

Height 1 m (3 ft). Raised by Meilland of France, this fine bedding rose was introduced in 1957. The blooms are deep velvety crimson, are of good shape and possess a slight fragrance. They tolerate rain very well indeed. Very free flowering and of vigorous growth. Otherwise as for nos. 227 and 228.

256. 'Lilli Marlene'
Floribunda

Height 75 cm (2½ ft). Yet another variety raised by Kordes. Introduced in 1959. The scarlet-red blooms are produced freely in large clusters and the colour does not fade. Usually healthy but a little mildew may appear. A compact upright bush, excellent for bedding. Otherwise as for no. 227.

257. 'Maria Callas'
Hybrid Tea

Height 1 m (3 ft). This was raised by Meilland and introduced in 1965. The large double flowers are very fragrant and are a very bright carmine-pink. They are freely produced on a vigorous bush. Otherwise as for nos. 227 and 228.

'Picasso'
Floribunda

Height 60 cm (2 ft). An unusual bedding rose raised by McGredy and introduced in 1971, when it caused much excitement. The basic colour is red but the blooms are splashed with white. A low-growing variety which can be thoroughly recommended for bedding. Otherwise as for no. 227.

258. 'McGredy's Sunset'
Hybrid Tea

Height 1 m (3 ft). This is a very old variety, being introduced in 1933 and, of course, raised by McGredy. It is probably being superseded nowadays by modern bicolored varieties such as 'Esther Ofarim', 'Piccadilly' and the like. Otherwise as for nos. 227 and 228.

259. 'Mischief'
Hybrid Tea

Height 1 m (3 ft). Raised by McGredy and introduced in 1960, this rose is extremely free flowering and has well-formed fragrant blooms. Disease free and very tolerant of hot sun or rain. Received the R.N.R.S. Presidents' International Trophy. Otherwise as for nos. 227 and 228.

260. 'Franklin Engelmann'
Floribunda

Height 1 m (3 ft). Raised by Dickson of Northern Ireland and introduced in 1970. This floribunda has very well-shaped bright scarlet blooms, almost of hybrid tea form, borne freely on a fairly large plant. Otherwise as for no. 227.

261. 'Pascali'
Hybrid Tea

Height 1 m (3 ft). Raised by Lens of Belgium and introduced in 1963. A very good white variety which opens its flowers in wet weather although it tends to have pale spots. Growth is sturdy and the blooms are carried on strong stems. A good cut flower and well recommended for bedding. Otherwise as for nos. 227 and 228.

'Virgo'
Hybrid Tea

Height 1 m (3 ft). This is a very famous white hybrid tea rose raised by Mallerin

and introduced in 1947. The slightly fragrant flowers appear very freely but they do not like much rain. The foliage is rather prone to mildew. Nevertheless a good bedder. Otherwise as for nos. 227 and 228.

262. 'Peace'
Hybrid Tea

Height 120–150 cm (4½–5 ft). One of the most famous of all roses, raised in France by Meilland and introduced in 1942. A very tall rose, free flowering with very large blooms, rain resistant and quite disease free. It needs room to spread its branches—the spread equals the height. Should be in every garden. Otherwise as for nos. 227 and 228.

263. 'Peer Gynt'
Hybrid Tea

Height 1 m (3 ft). Raised by Kordes and introduced in 1968. A very fine yellow hybrid tea. The blooms become slightly pink-tinted as they age. The large plants are well covered with deep green foliage, making a good background to the many blooms. Otherwise as for nos. 227 and 228.

264. 'Pink Peace'
Hybrid Tea

Height 120 cm (4 ft). A Meilland variety, like its famous parent, and introduced in 1959. The large blooms are bright pink and are very richly scented. This is a very healthy variety, useful for hedging or for large beds. Not everyone likes the intense colour but there is no doubt it makes a good display. Otherwise as for nos. 227 and 228.

RAMBLING AND CLIMBING ROSES

265. 'Aloha'

Large-flowered Climber

Height 2 m (6 ft). Raised by Boerner and introduced in 1955. The full, large, well-formed blooms are fragrant, very freely produced and are continuously borne during the summer. It is best grown up a pole or pillar, or on a wall or fence, or it could be grown as a large shrub. Climbing roses generally need little pruning. Simply cut out some of the old wood each year and then shorten the remaining young growths a little. Do not remove too much old wood at any one time as most climbers make new growth quite high up on this and it is this young wood that produces the flowers. Cut out any dead wood while pruning, which is best done in March. Keep the stems well tied in to supports. Otherwise climbers need the same cultural treatment as hybrid tea and floribunda roses. See no. 227.

266. 'Blaze'

Climber

Height 2·5–3 m (8–10 ft). This vigorous rose was raised by Kallay and introduced in 1932. The bright scarlet flowers are medium-sized and are carried in small clusters. Can be grown up pillars or posts or on walls and fences. Otherwise as for no. 265.

267. 'Danse des Sylphes'

Climber

Height 2·5–3 m (8–10 ft). This climber was raised by Mallerin and introduced in 1957. The bright orange-red, medium-sized rounded flowers are produced very freely in the summer and there is some recurrent blooming. A vigorous variety for pillar, post, wall or fence. Otherwise as for no. 265.

268. 'Danse du Feu'

Large-flowered Climber

Height 2·5 m (8 ft). Raised by Mallerin and introduced in 1954, this rose has moderately full, flattish blooms which are produced very freely throughout the summer. It can be grown on pillars or posts, but also suitable for training on walls and fences. Otherwise as for no. 265.

'Parkdirektor Riggers'

Kordesii Climber

Height 3 m (10 ft). This was raised in Germany by Wilhelm Kordes and introduced in 1957. The blood-red semi-double flowers, carried in clusters, are very freely produced. It is a repeat-flowering variety. Recommended for training on a wall or fence. Otherwise as for no. 265.

'Golden Showers'

Large-flowered Climber

Height 2–2·5 m (6–8 ft). Raised by Germaine, introduced in 1957, since when it has become a very popular golden-yellow climber. The large semi-double flowers are fragrant and are freely produced. This rose is repeat-flowering. Recommended for growing up a post or pillar or as a large free shrub. Otherwise as for no. 265.

'Mermaid'

Bracteata Climber

Height up to 6 m (20 ft). An old variety raised by Paul and introduced in 1917. A hybrid of *Rosa bracteata* and a tea rose. The very large single blooms are primrose yellow with amber-yellow stamens. It flowers all through the season. The blooms are fragrant.

Resents too much pruning. Grows on walls or fences. Otherwise as for no. 265.

'Ritter von Barmstede'
Kordesii Climber

Height 2–3 m (6–10 ft). Raised, of course, by Kordes, and introduced in 1960. The clusters of fully double, deep rose-pink flowers are quickly repeating on strong new shoots. This variety is very vigorous and has glossy disease-resistant foliage. Recommended as a pillar rose, or good for a fence. Otherwise as for no. 265.

269. 'Dorothy Perkins'
Rambler

Height up to 6 m (20 ft). Raised by Jackson and Perkins of United States and introduced in 1901. The small double rose-pink flowers in large clusters appear only for a few weeks in mid-summer. The plant is at the time smothered with blooms. It is an extremely vigorous variety and can be used for many purposes—pergolas, arches, screens, etc. It is very prone to mildew. However, it was immensely popular in the first half of this century, and, indeed, is still quite extensively planted by amateurs. Ramblers need different pruning from climbers. All the old stems are cut out at ground level as soon as flowering is over and the young canes are tied in in their place. These can be shortened a little if desired. Otherwise ramblers need the same cultural treatment as hybrid tea and floribunda roses. See no. 227.

270. 'Excelsa'
Rambler

Height 5·5 m (18 ft). Raised by Walsh, introduced in 1909. In mid-summer this rose produces large clusters of flowers on very vigorous stems. Abundant glossy foliage. Suitable for pergolas, arches, screens and so on. Otherwise as for no. 269.

271. 'Golden Rambler'
Rambler

Height 5·5 m (18 ft). Raised by Easlea and introduced in 1932, this rose is known also as 'Easlea's Golden Rambler'. The moderately large and full blooms are borne in small clusters amidst abundant olive-green foliage. Summer flowering, and ideal for pergolas, arches, etc. Otherwise as for no. 269.

272. 'Galway Bay'
Climber

Height 2·5–3 m (8–10 ft). A McGredy variety put out in 1966. The colour of the flowers holds until the petals fall and the blooms are very quick to repeat. An ideal variety for pillars, needing very little training. This one is very highly recommended. Otherwise as for no. 265.

273. 'Gloire de Dijon'
Large-flowered Climber

Height 4–4·5 m (13–15 ft). A very old variety appearing in 1853. Raised by Jacotot. The fragrant flowers appear in summer and there is usually a second flush in late summer. Although old, it is still often planted as it is a very fine rose; excellent on walls. Otherwise as for no. 265.

274. 'Heidelberg'
Modern Shrub Rose

Height 2–2·5 m (6–8 ft). A Kordes' variety introduced in 1958. Although this is a shrub rose it can be grown as a pillar rose when it will look very effective with its full, large, bright red flowers in trusses. These are freely produced and they repeat. Otherwise as for no. 265.

275. 'High Noon'
Semi-climber

Height 2 m (6 ft). Raised by Lammerts and introduced in 1946. The deep yellow semi-double flowers are fragrant and they repeat. This is not very vigorous but is very good for growing on pillars. Otherwise as for no. 265.

276. 'Handel'
Climber

Height 2·5 m (8 ft). Raised by McGredy of Ireland and appeared in 1965. The hybrid-tea type blooms are of unusual colour—cream, edged with bright pink. This rose blooms all through the summer and the growth is vigorous and upright. Good rain resistance. An excellent variety for a pillar. Otherwise as for no. 265.

277. 'New Dawn'
Rambler

Height 2·5 m (8 ft). Raised by Dreer, this rose appeared in 1930. This is a repeat-flowering rambler with flowers in a really delightful shade of pink. It makes a bushy specimen and can be grown on a pillar or post or on a fence. Although classed as a rambler, the new growths spring from older wood higher up the stems. Cut out one or two old stems occasionally to within 45 cm (18 in.) of the ground. Cut back old wood higher up to a good new leading shoot. Pruning can be done after flowering. Otherwise as for no. 227.

278. 'Sanders' White'
Rambler

Height 2·5–4 m (8–13 ft). Raised by Sanders and introduced in 1915. This is a very free-flowering variety with clusters of small, white, full blooms which have a very sweet scent. It is an all-purpose rose, suitable for pergolas, arches, screen, etc. Otherwise as for no. 269.

279. 'Sympathie'
Kordesii Climber

Height 3 m (10 ft). A superb Kordes' variety introduced in 1966. The very shapely blooms are scarlet. It is a vigorous plant and is very tough. Excellent for pillars, walls or fences. Otherwise as for no. 265.

CLIMBING PLANTS

280. Actinidia kolomikta
Height 3–6 m (10–20 ft). This climber is a native of China and Japan and is grown for its unusual green, pink and white leaves. The white flowers appear in June. The foliage only colours really well if the plant is grown on a south- or west-facing wall in full sun. It is a twining plant and will need some extra support such as a trellis or horizontal wires. Provide a good, fertile, loamy soil. Propagation is from seed or from moderately ripened cuttings rooted in a warm frame.

281. Aristolochia durior
Dutchman's Pipe

Height 4·5–9 m (15–30 ft). A native of eastern North America. This is a twining plant suitable for covering walls, fences and large tree stumps and it can also be grown in trees or up pergolas, arches and so on. It does not mind being in sun or shade but it likes a reasonably fertile soil to give of its best. The large kidney-shaped leaves are quite attractive but it is the flowers which are most remarkable. These really do resemble a pipe and they are green in colour with a brownish-purple mouth. They are produced in June. Despite its exotic appearance it is quite hardy in Britain. This climber can be pruned during the winter to keep it within bounds. Cuttings will root quite easily in coarse sand in a warm frame..

282.   Campsis radicans
Trumpet Vine

Height up to 9 m (30 ft). This spectacular plant comes from the south-eastern United States. It is excellent on walls or large tree stumps and pergolas but it needs to be grown in full sun to ripen its growth and produce the orange and scarlet trumpet-shaped flowers. Therefore choose a south-facing wall for your plant. This climber clings to walls, etc., by means of aerial roots but it may need some additional support in the early stages of growth. The blooms appear in August/September. Grow in good well-drained soil. Thin out growths if necessary in late February or March. Propagate from seed, woody cuttings, suckers or root cuttings.

283.   Celastrus scandens
False or Shrubby Bitter-sweet

Height up to 6 m (20 ft). A native of North America. This twining plant is very vigorous and is useful for covering old walls (where it will need extra supports), hedges, trees and so on. It will grow in full sun or shade and in any ordinary garden soil. The main attraction of this plant is the crop of fruits produced in autumn by female plants, though this species is not very free fruiting in Britain. A better species is

Celastrus orbiculatus, 9–12 m (30–40 ft), from north-east Asia. This produces an abundance of red and yellow fruits and also in the autumn the leaves turn to clear yellow. Prune in winter to keep within bounds. Propagate from layers or seed.

284.   Clematis montana rubens

Height 6–9 m (20–30 ft). From western and central China. This is one of the small-flowered clematis and it produces a mass of pink flowers during May and June. It is very vigorous and can be grown on large walls (where it will need the additional support of horizontal wires), over sheds and outhouses, or up trees or pergolas. It will thrive in any aspect and is particularly suitable for a north-facing wall. It likes its roots in cool, moist, but well-drained soil. Roots can be kept shaded and cool with a flat stone or two, or with low-growing shrubs, like lavender. Enrich soil with well-rotted manure before planting. Usually supplied in pots. When planting disturb the rootball as little as possible, and plant deeply and firmly. In summer feed regularly with liquid fertiliser to encourage really good growth. Annual pruning of this clematis is not necessary, but if it gets unduly out of hand it can be cut back to within a few inches of the oldest wood when flowering is over. The easiest method of propagation for the amateur is layering in early summer. A good white-flowered variety of Clematis montana is grandiflora from China.

285.   Clematis vitalba
Old Man's Beard, Traveller's Joy

Height up to 12 m (40 ft). This is a native of Europe (including Britain) and North Africa. In Britain it is a common sight in the hedgerows, especially in the chalky areas of southern England. The almond-scented white flowers are produced from July to September and are followed by attractive feathery seed heads (285 a). This species is only recommended for those with a wild area in their garden as it is far too rampant for the average plot. It can be grown over large bushes or into trees. Little or no pruning needed, unless it gets out of hand. Otherwise as for no. 284.

286. Clematis hybrids

These are the large-flowered clematis which are so popular with amateur gardeners for growing on walls, arches, pergolas and so on, in any aspect. Cultivation as for no. 284, though pruning may differ. 'Comtesse de Bouchaud' (286 a) grows 3 m (10 ft) high and blooms continuously from June to September. Prune annually by cutting back in February all but 3 cm (1 in.) of the previous season's growths. 'Jackmanii' (286 b) is 6 m (20 ft) tall and its violet-blue flowers are produced continuously from June to September. Pruning as for no. 286 a. 'Nelly Koster' (286 c) is a pearly-white variety up to 4·5 m (15 ft) tall, and blooming from July to September. The blooms are translucent and have a mauve-pink bar on the reverse. Pruning as for no. 286 a. 'Nelly Moser' (286 d), 3 m (10 ft) high, flowers in May/June and again in September. Little pruning needed. Space out main growths annually. 'Mrs Hope' (286 e) attains 4·5 m (15 ft) in height and blooms in July/August. Pruning as for no. 286 a. 'The President' (286 f), 3 m (10 ft) tall, flowers June/July and September. Annual training as for no. 286 d. 'Ville de Lyon' (286 g), 3 m (10 ft), blooms from July to September. Prune as for no. 286 a.

287. Clematis tangutica

Height 3 m (10 ft). This species is a native of China. It is very easily grown and has attractive divided sea-green leaves and yellow lantern-shaped flowers in the autumn. Highly recommended for low walls, trellis work, fences and the like. There is a good variety called 'Gravetye'. Both have attractive silky seed heads after the flowers. Pruning can consist of cutting the plant back to 90–120 cm (3 or 4 ft) in February. Otherwise as for no. 284.

288. Clematis viticella

Height 3–4 m (10–13 ft). This species is a native of south-east Europe. The fragrant blooms are produced from July to September. There is a number of good forms of this clematis such as 'Alba Luxurians', white; 'Minuet', creamy white, banded purple; and 'Royal Velours', deep velvety purple. Prune in February by cutting back all but 2½ cm (1 in.) of the previous season's growths. Otherwise as for no. 284.

289. Clematis viticella 'Kermesina'

Height 3–4 m (10–13 ft). A very good variety of the above species with deep wine-crimson flowers. It blooms freely from July to September. Otherwise as for no. 288.

290. Hydrangea petiolaris
Climbing Hydrangea

Height 18–25 m (60–80 ft). This vigorous climber is a native of Japan. It clings by aerial roots and is ideal for covering walls, fences, outbuildings, etc. Especially suitable for growing on a shady north-facing wall. The white lacecap flowers are produced in June. It will grow in any ordinary garden soil. In its early stages of growth it may need some support until its aerial roots take a good hold. No pruning needed, except to keep it within bounds. Propagate from cuttings.

291. Jasminum nudiflorum
Winter Jasmine

Height 4 m (13 ft). This is a Chinese climber which is very popular in British gardens. It is valued for its cheerful yellow flowers which appear from November to February on the bare stems. Usually trained against a wall or fence. The main stems will need tying in to wires or trellis. Pruning consists of cutting back the side shoots which have flowered almost to the main stems. The new side shoots should be left intact as they will flower the following year. Prune immediately after flowering each year. This jasmine will thrive in any aspect and any well-drained soil. Excellent choice for industrial areas. Shoots in bud will quickly open their flowers if cut and placed in water in a warm room. Propagate from cuttings in August.

292. Lonicera caprifolium
Perfoliate Honeysuckle

Height 3–6 m (10–20 ft). A native of Europe which is found growing wild in England. The fragrant flowers are produced in June and July. Ideal for growing over large bushes or tree stumps and up trees, pergolas, arches or trelliswork. Thrives in most soils and enjoys semi-shade, though equally happy in full sun if roots are shaded. It is a twining plant. If it becomes overgrown, shorten current season's shoots to within five buds of their base during September. Propagate from August cuttings.

293. Lonicera × heckrotii

Height 2–3 m (6–10 ft). This is probably a hybrid between Lonicera × americana and Lonicera sempervirens. Origin uncertain. A shrubby honeysuckle which also climbs. The flowers are fragrant and appear from June to August. A very free-flowering kind. Suitable for growing against small supports or over tree stumps. Otherwise as for no. 292.

294. Lonicera henryi

Height 3–5 m (10–16 ft). A native of China, this species is evergreen or semi-evergreen in Britain. It is very vigorous and produces its blooms in June and July. These are followed by black fruits. Otherwise as for no. 292.

295. Lonicera periclymenum
Woodbine

Height 3–6 m (10–20 ft). This well-known honeysuckle comes from Europe, North Africa and Asia Minor. The blooms are very fragrant and appear from June to August. They are followed by clusters of red fruits (295 a). It is a very common wild plant in Britain and is often seen scrambling over large bushes and hedges. It has two varieties which are, perhaps, better for growing in the garden. One is the Early Dutch Honeysuckle, Lonicera periclymenum 'Belgica', which blooms during May and June and again in late summer. The other is the Late Dutch Honeysuckle, Lonicera periclymenum 'Serotina', and this flowers from July to October. Both are scented. Otherwise as for no. 292.

296. Lonicera × tellmanniana

Height 3–4 m (10–13 ft). This is a hybrid between Lonicera tragophylla and Lonicera sempervirens. It is one of the finest climbing honeysuckles for garden cultivation and the bright yellow and copper flowers are freely produced in June and July. They are not fragrant, unfortunately. It grows best in semi-shade or even in full shade. The upper leaves are perfoliate, in other words the basal lobes are united around the stem. Otherwise as for no. 292.

297. Parthenocissus quinquefolia
Virginia Creeper

Height 6–8 m (20–26 ft). A vigorous climber from eastern North America whose leaves take on rich crimson tints in the autumn. It is then a gorgeous sight on the walls of large houses. It supports itself by adhesive pads which are located on tendrils. It will thrive in any aspect and likes most ordinary garden soils provided they are well drained. No pruning is necessary unless you wish to trim it to keep it within bounds. Do this in winter. Propagate from cuttings in late summer.

298. Parthenocissus tricuspidata
Boston Ivy

Height 8-10 m (26–33 ft). A native of China and Japan. This is another self-clinging species, supporting itself by means of adhesive pads on tendrils. Suitable for growing on larger walls. The leaves turn rich crimson and scarlet in the autumn. The fruits are dark blue and covered with 'bloom'. The leaves are variable in shape. There is a form called *Parthenocissus tricuspidata* 'Veitchii' which has slightly smaller leaves. These are purple when they are young. Both are very good climbers for town gardens. Otherwise as for no. 297.

299. Polygonum baldschuanicum
Russian Vine

Height up to 12 m (40 ft). A native of southern Turkestan. This is one of the most rampant climbers available in Britain, where it is used to quickly cover large walls, sheds and outhouses, oil storage tanks, old trees, or indeed any unsightly object. The panicles of white flowers are very attractive and are produced freely between July and October. Any soil and aspect. Can be cut back hard if required. Propagate from heel cuttings of half-ripe wood in July/August in a warm frame, or from hard-wood cuttings in autumn.

300. Wisteria sinensis
Chinese Wisteria

Height up to 30 m (100 ft). A native of China, this beautiful twining plant produces its pendulous flowers in May. It can be trained on walls, pergolas, arches and so on, and also looks well growing into a large tree. Easily trained to any shape by spacing out and tying in young stems to form a permanent framework of branches. Annual pruning is necessary: in August cut back all young side shoots (unless needed for training) on the main stems to about 30 cm (12 in.); then in winter further reduce these to 8 cm (3 in.). Wisterias must have full sunshine and they will grow best of all in a deep fertile soil. Propagate by layering shoots in summer.

301–302. Vitis vinifera
Grape Vine

Height up to 15 m (50 ft). A native of the Caucasus region, and hardy in the British Isles. The Grape Vine supports itself by means of tendrils. It can be grown on arches and pergolas, or walls provided horizontal wires are erected so that the stems can be tied in. Vines are very decorative and can be trained to any shape, and of course the berries can be eaten. The berries of some make very good wine. They succeed in a deep fertile soil and full sun. Pruning consists of shortening back side shoots (on the main framework of branches) once or twice during the summer, and shortening them hard back in the winter. One of the most popular varieties in Britain for outdoor cultivation is 'Brant' with bunches of sweet, aromatic, purple-black grapes suitable for wine. The leaves turn deep red and purple in the autumn. Two varieties are illustrated in this book: the black-fruited 'Black Cluster (301) and the white-fruited 'Early Malingre' (302). Propagation from cuttings of well-ripened shoots inserted out of doors in October. The cuttings should contain two or three buds, and only the top bud should show above soil level after insertion. When preparing a cutting, cut just below a bud at the base, and just above a bud at the top.

INDEX OF LATIN NAMES

(Numbers refer both to colour plates and to descriptive notes. Where an illustration is not numbered the page number is given.)

INDEX OF ENGLISH NAMES

(Numbers refer both to colour plates and to descriptive notes. Where an illustration is not numbered the page number is given.)